MW00415478

CORAL COMES HIGH

GEORGE P. HUNT
U. S. MARINE CORPS RESERVE

With a Foreword by
GENERAL ALEXANDER A. VANDEGRIFT

TABLE OF CONTENTS

FOREWORD

IN A very real sense the history of the United States Marines might be told as a series of separate and collective incidents wherein relatively small forces of men accomplished specific tasks. Although the Marines have operated as an integral part of large strategic forces — particularly in the winning of the war in the Pacific it is nevertheless true that, in the final analysis, the battle is won by the individual fighting man operating as a member of a squad, a platoon, a company. In an over-all sense there must be an esprit de corps and a larger organization under competent senior officers, but in the individual task, the individual incident, the leadership is up to the junior officer and the noncommissioned officer. The association must be that of men who have an individual respect for one another and a reliance on themselves, their comrades and their leaders. In the heat of battle a man cannot stop to think about the larger ideal; he must fight with courage and resourcefulness because his own life and his self-respect (without which few men can live) depend upon association with, and the respect of, his comrades.

It is my belief that Captain George Hunt has told here a story which is important in the history of the United States Marines. It is not an official account, and Captain Hunt has not attempted to give an overall picture of grand strategy, nor even the complete story of Peleliu. He has, however, told in the simplest terms the story of his own company — a small force which suffered terrible casualties and fought against considerable odds to see a specific job through. If this small unit, this small association of fighting men, had not done its job, there is no knowing what the results might have been in terms of casualties along an entire beach sector. Captain Hunt has been awarded the Navy Cross as commander of a company of Marine riflemen on Peleliu. This is a story of fighting men told by a fighting man.

ALEXANDER A. VANDEGRIFT
General, United States Marine Corps
January, 1946

INTRODUCTION

AT 0830, September 15, 1944, the First Marine Division attacked the Japanese-held island of Peleliu in the Palau Islands and engaged an estimated 10,000 Japanese in one of the fiercest straggles of the war. This division consisted of three infantry regiments, the First, the Fifth, and the Seventh, one artillery regiment, the Eleventh, a headquarters battalion and numerous attached units such as a battalion of tanks, amphibious tractors, engineers, and pioneers. Commanding the division was Major General William H. Rupertus.

My regiment, the First, according to military organization, consisted of a headquarters and service company, a heavy weapons company and three battalions, the First, the Second, and the Third. It was commanded by Colonel Louis B. Puller whose executive officer, or next in command, was Lieutenant Colonel R. P. Ross, Jr. My battalion, the Third, divided into a headquarters company and three rifle companies lettered "I," "K," and "L," was commanded by Lieutenant Colonel Stephen V. Sabol whose executive officer was Major William McNulty. I was in command of Company "K" with an organization consisting of a headquarters platoon, which contained a section of three sixty-millimeter mortars and command and supply groups, three rifle platoons, the first, second and third, and a machine-gun platoon. In no sense is this hook the complete account of the Peleliu invasion. It is principally a story of my company and myself and what happened to us during a grim action of forty-eight hours' duration. With one exception, I have used the real names of real persons.

    G.H.

PROLOGUE

LATE one hot August night we, a company of marines, were winding in a column of twos through the shadowy darkness of a coconut grove, between the rigid and scarcely visible tree trunks. We wore helmets and battle gear and carried on our shoulders canvas rolls containing extra clothing and bedding. Under the weight we bent forward as we walked. Most of us were silent, but a few were talking in subdued tones. We were sweating, and our jackets, wet under our packs, were clinging uncomfortably to our backs. Our movements made muffled sounds; trouser legs slapping against each other, a canteen clinking where it did not fit snugly in the drinking cup, rifle butts scraping against cartridge belts. Occasionally someone's foot would strike a stone or a log or the roots of a fallen tree or sink into a hole of sucking mud, and a muttered curse would follow.

We came to a dirt road that bordered the coconut grove. By night it appeared as a blue strip cutting through the blackness which shrouded the trees. We turned left toward the bay, and saw scattered orange lights on the shore. As we approached the beach road which ran perpendicular to our route, we saw the hulking shapes of trucks and tanks and tractors jammed together and interlocked in the initial confusion that accompanied the loading of ships in preparation for an assault landing.

Our column emerged from the darkness inland into the dim light and the turmoil on the beach. It halted as it confronted the massive, steel barrier of tanks that blocked its way. Men with flashlights were attempting to direct this lumbersome traffic, but the roar of idling engines drowned out their orders. Men stripped to the waist were climbing out of the turrets of tanks, out of the cabs of Alligators and ten-wheel trucks loaded with crates, pointing vigorously at each other, their mouths wide open with shouts and invectives that went unheard or unheeded.

Down the column we passed the word from man to man; "Take a break; smoking lamp is lit." We slowly dispersed into the shadows on either side of the road, and the darkness there was pin-pointed by the flares of our matches and the glowing ends of our cigarettes.

In an hour or so this confusion on the beach would straighten itself out Then we would board ship, and our immediate future would be sealed. The reason for our existence would be confined entirely to one objective, and there would be no respite until that objective was attained.

PART ONE: BEFORE LANDING

CHAPTER ONE

SHE sat like a squat, sedentary old maid. Flat-bottomed and broad of beam, she seemed motionless except for the thin curl of foam at her waterline. Dirty green and black camouflage had been smeared on her sides, and rust spread toward the top of her blunt bow, across her huge white numerals. As with an old tanker, her main deck was the forward two-thirds of her length. On the remaining third aft rose a stubby superstructure with a boat deck, a wheel-house and a canvas-covered conn where the skipper sat on a high stool with a speaking tube and a compass in front of him. The rigid lines of her boxlike hull were abruptly broken at the bow by the peculiar upward surge of the foc'sle surmounted by two open, circular turrets. Placidly resting on the water she appeared to be a peaceful, harmless ship, except for the long thin guns which bristled on her decks and pointed threateningly skyward.

Around her were many similar ships, all formed in even columns, all turning on the zig and the zag of their course in one lumbering motion, all inching ahead at seven knots. Toward the horizon were the protecting destroyers, rakish and jaunty, cruising back and forth around the fringes of the convoy. Sometimes their sleek hulls were lost in the graying atmosphere, and only the white foam at their bows showed that they were there.

The ocean was flat and gray and with the leaden sky above trapped the suffocating heat, mirrored it, increasing its intensity. Tomorrow a squall or perhaps a cool steady wind from the northeast? Doubtful — during September in these parts a typhoon was the only possible variation.

A dark chunk on this endless expanse of water, LST 227 was war-weary and seemed to resent each knot that slipped under her stern. Dully submissive she plodded along, a veteran, needing a new coat of paint, a new gyro and an overhauling in a dry dock. Since she had sailed down the Mississippi on her maiden voyage to the Gulf of Mexico, through the Canal into the Pacific, she had seen Kwajalein, Hollandia, Guam, Tinian, and now, with Truk off her stern, she was again far into Japanese waters bound for Peleliu, the last of the steppingstones to the Philippines.

She was heavy with cargo; trucks and jeeps, and water trailers, amphibian tractors, a distillation unit, and crates of kettles, pots, ladles and rations, ammunition, explosives, drums of water, oil and gasoline. Heavy seas would swamp her; a hit by a Japanese bomb would touch off the explosives and blow her to a thousand pieces. She was relying heavily on the protecting umbrella to be furnished at a moment's notice by the three flattops whose outlines were dim on the horizon far astern.

When we first boarded No. 227 we had the usual difficulty of crowding ourselves into the limited living space which the Navy provided for us. The sleeping compartments down below accommodated only 77 and since there were 235 in my company, the others spilled over the main deck, finding what living space they could in the confusion of trucks and jeeps and water trailers and drums and piles of crates. All these were lashed to each other and to the deck by an intricate network of chains and braces. Through these countless barriers was one narrow passageway running fore and aft on the port side. The only obstacles on it were an occasional knee-high chain and the topside showers which it just managed to circumvent though still well within splashing range.

More as protection from the sun than from the rain we hoisted up huge, green tarpaulins. Underneath them the men slung their jungle hammocks fastening the suspending ropes to any available object that was sturdy enough. They unfolded cots wherever they could make them fit, and before long everyone at least had a covered place to sleep. But moving around for anything but the necessary functions of living was impossible.

Amidships and perched precariously on top of a loaded track above the level of the tarpaulins was one isolated cot covered by a camouflaged poncho angled across four tent poles like the canopy over a throne. The owner of this home was sitting on the cot cleaning his rifle, majestically oblivious to the turmoil which seethed beneath him.

The days and nights rolled into each other, losing their delineations of time. The murky, equatorial heat would muffle the sound of voice? and the rattling of mess gear as the men formal the chow line on the port side. The PA system would croak "first platoon chow!" and the line would move slowly aft toward the galley. The third platoon would be just finishing taking showers, and the spray, splattering off the sun-browned backs of the men, would splash the chow line. For a moment there would be congestion as the two lines merged, then straightened themselves out as they crisscrossed and filed off in different directions. The food was comparatively edible, as it usually was in the Navy, with occasional helpings of roast beef and fresh string beans.

Afternoon would drone by with a game of hearts, a shabby, well-thumbed pocket mystery, an hour's schooling and exercise on the boat deck, cleaning a rifle, evening chow and sick call down below where the heat was so oppressive that even the exercise of breathing made you sweat. The night would cool slightly, and the sky would swarm with stars. At one signal blackout would transform the convoy to ghost ships. The mornings would drag on like the afternoons, except that there would always be the rarely realized possibility of having fresh eggs for breakfast.

With Peleliu only three days away we began to think of our hopes for the future. The hours ticking by carried us to something which none of us knew about, but of which many had deep thoughts. Nearness of death produces varied personal philosophies. Some men challenge and defy death, some develop a fatalistic gloom, some are oblivious to it, some are cheerful and confident, some have faith in God and believe implicitly in His protection. At odd moments I have heard men express their thoughts on the subject. "When my number is up, there isn't much I can do about it. You know, three strikes and you're out."

"I haven't any number. The bastards might nick me but they'll never kill me."

"To hell with it. You either 'get it' or you don't, so why worry. If I 'get it' I hope it's quick."

"Whenever I begin to worry too much about it I go to church services and come back feeling much better."

I have often heard men say after a battle, "Joe got it in the head. Somehow I had a feeling he would, and I remember he told me once that he thought he'd never make it." Sometimes such premonitions come true — inexplicably — though usually they have no more meaning than mere superficial remarks. An officer whom I knew quite well had always been a hard luck kid. He invariably studied the wrong paragraphs for his examinations in college and consequently received very low marks. His best girl turned him down. He could never make the grade in athletics, and when he played cards his luck went against him. He was not strongly built, rather pale and thin. On Guadalcanal when I heard that he had been killed I was shocked but not surprised. Somehow I had expected it

An exceptionally close friend of mine told me the evening before we landed on New Britain that he knew he was going to be killed. It was not long after the first shots had been fired that I saw him carried out on a stretcher with the telltale pallor on his face. Another who landed on Guadalcanal with me believed so completely in an inevitable death that he wrote his epitaph for his college magazine before leaving the States. He was shot through the head by a Jap lieutenant.

On the other hand, one of my sergeants on New Britain had a strong premonition of death and took incredible chances, as though to say, "Come on, let's get it over with." It never came. But many times I have seen men who were continually smiling and happy and never had a morose moment, who defied death, who prayed to God for protection from it or who naively believed that it could not touch them, suddenly blown to bits by a mortar shell or riddled by machine-gun bullets. These are the unfortunate majority of fatalities, victims of the normal happenings of war from which death is as inseparable as life from the beating of the heart.

Whatever our deeper feelings regarding our future we adopted, through training and necessity, a mental attitude of cold professionalism as though to say: It's just another day. But the usual physical signs of prebattle tension began to appear as we crept very near to our objective.

Laughter was often too loud and frequent; silences seemed too still; trivialities became major issues. There was a hushed atmosphere of preparedness exaggerated now by what had been so unchanging since we left our base in the Russells; the monotonous throb of the engines, sultry, stultifying heat, the drab overtones of ocean and sky and loneliness in the midst of vast space.

CHAPTER TWO

WE HAD been told that this campaign would be "short and snappy." Peleliu was a very small island, an area of some eight square miles, and once the First Division landed, there would be no room for the Japs and ourselves, as there had been for so many months on Guadalcanal and New Britain. We expected a quick, sharp fight which meant, as my lanky first sergeant remarked in his Tennessee twang, "We'll have to kill every little yellow bastard there." The division had called a center rush aimed directly at the airfield which once in our hands would protect MacArthur s right flank when he struck the Philippines. The airfield was situated on the southern flatland of the island which bulged there to a width of about two miles. The northern sector was a narrow, curving peninsula split by jagged, bald ridges running north and south. The Fifth Regiment was to seize the airfield, elements of the Seventh were to clear the area south of the airfield, and the First was to land on the left of the Fifth, smash into the ridges, turn to the north and mop up the entire peninsula. The landing beaches were all on the western coast. My battalion, the Third, was the left assault unit of the regiment, and my company, Company K, was the left assault unit of the battalion. Thus we were on the extreme left of the entire divisional operation, and after one look at the map we realized that we were liable to meet tough opposition. We were hoping for another Kwajalein, but no one denied that it could be a Tarawa or a Saipan or worse.

On the immediate left of our landing beach, designated as Beach White, there was a point of land which, by measuring on the map, jutted into the water about twenty-five yards. From this strategic position the Japs could murderously rake the entire beach with as much fire power as they chose to put there. Since aerial photographs showed anti-boat obstacles on the coral reef in front of the beach, entrenchments on the beach and two pillboxes on the Point, it appeared that the Japs were taking full advantage of the terrain. From where we were to land this Point was about fifty yards to our left, and if it was at all active we would be caught in a deathtrap, swept by flanking fire at point-blank range. After landing we were to turn ninety degrees to the north with our left flank anchored on the beach, fan out inland and attack to the first objective (0-1). The Point, marking the eastern end of 0-1, was in the left of my company sector. Thus my company would act as the pivot for the turning movement to the north of the battalion and the entire regiment. Stated in the written order our mission ran: "Seize 0-1 and proceed to 0-2 on order." "Seize 0-1," an easy statement but how easy to accomplish?

We hoped that, as it happened at Kwajalein, the naval shelling and bombing would be so devastating that it would drive the Japs deep in their holes, paralyzed and half crazy from concussion, and fix them there until we swarmed over their shattered positions. When we heard that the Navy was to start a concentrated shelling three days before our landing, and bombing ten days before, we thought that perhaps our hope would be realized.

My aim in planning a scheme of maneuver was to mass the most at the right place at the right time. So, figuring that the Point was the "right place," I gave my third rifle platoon the job of assaulting it and put the first in support directly Behind the third with the primary mission to be ready to reinforce at a moment's notice. I placed the second platoon on the right with the mission of assaulting that half of my sector. My machine-gun platoon, organized into three sections, I split up with one section supporting each of the two assault platoons and the third held in support Thus, considering the disposition of my units, I had "the most" directed against the Point which was the key terrain feature in my sector. As for "the right time," that would be determined by the progress of the fight and when I committed the first platoon.

Four times we had rehearsed this maneuver, traced it on the map over and over again until every man in the company knew what he was supposed to do and where he was supposed to do it in relation to the man next to him. But, as on the opening night of the most well-rehearsed play, an actor may miss his entrance, the leading man may stumble on his lines or the audience may be embarrassingly unreceptive. Fighting is confusion. When forces have met in conflict events move so swiftly that control is reduced to a minimum. Casualties deplete the mass. The plan may be refuted by the unforeseen, and even the misstep of one individual may change the best-laid scheme or completely alter the expected sequence of battle. The counter to these elements of confusion is iron-clad organization, flexible enough within its structure to meet quickly and successfully any situation, capable of smart teamwork and spirited by tough-minded aggressiveness.

If any portion of my plan was to break down, the seizure of the Point must not. Should we fail to capture and hold the Point the entire regimental beach would be exposed to heavy fire from the flank. We were proud of our responsibility, and every man in the company was determined to fulfill it.

CHAPTER THREE

NORMALLY I am not superstitious, but during our weary days on 227 something happened which I could not help considering a gloomy omen. One of the men brought a little dog aboard whom he called "Bomber." Bomber was jet-black, smooth-haired and had a round head with mischievous eyes and a blunt nose. His parentage was suspiciously Japanese as his mother had wandered into our camp one evening on New Britain half starved and trembling with cold. Who had been responsible for her pregnancy we never knew, as it could have been any one of the stray mutts that used to appear from nowhere and find lodging in our galleys or in the vicinity of our garbage pits. We had all become very fond of Bomber with his quick, jerky mannerisms. One of the sailors aboard owned a larger dog, also of probable Jap descent, which he had picked up at Hollandia. It was reminiscent of an Airedale with a shaggy, matted coat, bowlegs and villainous eyes lodged in a foxlike head. One afternoon I got the word that the big dog had pushed Bomber overboard during a scuffle on the fantail. The commander of the flotilla immediately flashed a message to an escorting LCI to make a thorough search of the waters. The LCI veered from the column and started off on her mission at full speed. She searched until the approach of dusk, and when she flashed a negative report with her blinker, I felt vaguely uneasy about what lay ahead.

D-1 Day dawned startlingly clear, and a noticeable breeze was blowing from the north. The sea was chopped and sparkling from countless reflections. By sunup the day's program was in full swing. The tarpaulins were being unlashed, slipping into crazy angles, humped and puffed by the wind as the men struggled to fold them into neat squares. Hammocks were unslung and with all the personal belongings and excess equipment which would not be needed for fighting, were rolled into horseshoe-shaped bundles and stowed up forward. Again and again the deck was swept and swabbed in a futile effort to comply with the Navy's cleaning routine. Weapons were stripped down, and the parts were brushed with old toothbrushes and carefully oiled. Flame-throwers and bazookas were painted with new camouflage, and after the tedious rigmarole of obtaining the Navy's permission, a machine gun was test-fired over the side.

Khaki had been packed away the day before, and the men wore their battle dress: gray-green trousers and jacket with a black Marine Corps emblem stamped on the left breast pocket. The men were lean and wiry, their muscles prominent under their skin which was well tanned by the sun. Their hair was clipped short, and their squarely chiseled faces showed their determination to finish the ugly job which lay ahead of them as quickly as possible. About their eyes was the expression of experience or the quest for it. Among the 235 of Company K were every type, tall and short, stocky and thin, fair and dark, but unifying them into one driving spirit was an unshakable loyalty to each other, a unity far deeper than mere comradeship, and governed by a stern, silent code of mutual respect which could not be broken by a man in battle without his incurring the humiliating contempt of former friends. This was a force that would never allow them to let each other down and that would impel them to perform acts of bravery which, in the normal circumstances of peace, would seem incredible.

Most of my men were under twenty years old, and although some had grown cynical of military life, they were all extremely proud of their unit as a company and of their own individual and common strength and toughness which they knew would never be beaten. The great illusion of fighting a glorious war they had forgotten or had never known. Although they might have been stirred once by a parade, a cheering crowd and a brass band, they knew now that fighting was a dirty business in which the glamour that might have existed once in their imagination was lost. The veterans knew it, and they told the beginners. Their spirit was not heroic dash cluttered with moral mush, war bond salesmanship and political red herrings, but a solid bond of loyalty and mutual respect, tightened by the same hardships, the same likes and dislikes and the same fight for something which they had taken for granted three years ago but which now had suddenly become tremendously important — their lives.

I had often asked some of them why they were fighting and invariably received some such reply as, "It beats me," or "To get it over with and get home." Corporal Hahn expressed it more completely. He spoke very earnestly. "All I want is to go home to my wife, get my job back driving the mail truck, and be left alone." I asked him what prompted him to enlist in the service. "I don't know, exactly," he replied, "I do know that my father went through hell in the last war. He was gassed and still has to go to the hospital now and then to be treated. So I figured that if Dad, after going through what he did, would want his son to go through the same thing, there must be something in it. And some of my buddies were joining up too. So I joined up."

It seems to me that his answer conveyed the deep-rooted loyalty which can bind the members of a family to each other, to their home and their way of life in their community. This and the pressure of maintaining one's self-respect and the respect of one's fellow men, are the principal factors that motivate one to enlist, to fight and to continue to fight and possibly to die. Though less apparent, these are the same basic feelings as those which stirred the men of my company.

The morning's bustling activity came as a relief from the dreary routine of the voyage. It snapped the tension. All the training and the schooling and the planning were behind us. Our equipment was in good shape. We were ready.

Early in the afternoon I assembled the company just forward of the superstructure for a final summing up. Using the ship's public address system which produced a disconcerting crackling, I attempted to say the right thing. My speech could not be a "do or die," locker-room pep talk. Too much was at stake. It could only be a confident statement of our intentions with a practical note of encouragement. I mentioned that a powerful Navy was behind us, already laying down the heaviest bombardment in its history, that the Fifth Air Force had been bombing Peleliu for many days, and described some of the most recent information on Japanese installations on our beach. I finished with the theme that I had been pounding for three months, "Hit the beach and drive in fast for one hundred yards and keep driving; clear it for the succeeding waves." If the Japs were there, your momentum would send them reeling, and you would be clear of their mortars.

On a heavily defended beach many would get hurt, but it was the only way. The beachhead must be established. The men were silent when I ended my talk. They asked no questions; they had heard the same thing before. I wondered then if they were thinking as I was that some of us would probably not be around after it was over.

The company burlesque team, Rowe and O'Brien, relieved me of the microphone and put on a half hour's entertainment. Very soon the men were smiling and laughing to the gags of "The March of Slime," a recitation by Rowe and illustrative actions by O'Brien of "Casey at the Bat," Wisecracks at dog faces, the USO and defense strikers who were dissatisfied with ninety dollars a week brought an uproarious mixture of laughter, cheers and boos. Then Rowe, sounding amazingly like Walter Winchell, read the news of the blistering attack of "Bull" Halsey's task force in the vicinity of the Palau Islands. The skipper of the ship wished us God speed, and we closed the little ceremony.

After supper we held church services on the foc'sle among the oil drums. It was very peaceful there; the sky was clear blue-green, the ocean as blue as ink and the horizon ahead was beginning to radiate gold. A cool, gentle wind blew across the bow. There were only about forty of us clustered in a circle around a sailor who had lacked two years of graduating from divinity school when he joined the Navy and was acting as chaplain. The Gospel was read, and we recital the 2jrd Psalm and sang "Onward Christian Soldiers." As we were beginning "Abide with Me," I noticed, to my surprise, light drops of water appearing on my hands. I looked above and felt a thin rain on my face falling from a cloudless sky, and by the time we had finished the hymn it fell harder in larger drops drenching our heads and shoulders. Again I looked up but could only see a clear expanse of blue. In that strange rain which fell from nowhere we said the Lord's Prayer and completed the service.

In the wardroom that evening my six officers and I played our usual cutthroat game of hearts. I will always remember that last game, because many days later when we sat down for another under very different circumstances, two places were empty. The game was progressing unfavorably for "Bull" Sellers, my next in command. The black lady was haunting him all evening, and he would bellow in his deep Alabamian, "Gawd damn these cards, I never have received such a 'shaftin'!" His mustache seemed to bristle, and his big shoulders heaved back in his chair in disgust. Hanson, who led my mortar section, small, dirty blond and quiet, slouched in his seat and held his winning position as low man. On his left was Willis who had the first platoon, leaning shrewdly forward, intent on the game, his long nose and high forehead emphasizing his appearance of intentness. Occasionally he chided Sellers with "Well, well, Bull boy, how's it going? All set for another needle?" Next to him was Stramel who led my machine-gun platoon, tremendous and athletic, always unperturbed, playing his hand stolidly but not craftily; then Estey of the third platoon, black-headed, white-skinned, whose gay spirit and laughter were contagious to the rest of us. Woodyard who led my second platoon never joined us in these sessions but sat at the next table reading a book. That evening, he turned in early and I happened to look up to see his stocky figure disappear in the darkened gangway. "Good night, Woody!" I called after him. He turned around; his face was half lost in the shadows.

"Good night, Skipper."

Under the dim orange light, shrouded by cigarette smoke, the heart game continued until ten-thirty when we decided that Hanson had pocketed enough of our nickels. We sat around for another cup of coffee, and then, one by one, wandered off to bed. I doubted that I would be able to sleep well that night, but soon after stretching out on my bunk I dropped into a deep slumber.

PART TWO: LANDING

CHAPTER FOUR

I AWAKENED the next morning with a start. My sleep had been so heavy that it was not before I had thoroughly rubbed my eyes that I knew where I was and what an important day in my life this one was likely to be. Lying there drenched in sweat and drowsily conscious of the thumping of running feet on the deck above my head, the creaking of davits and pulleys and the whirring of the fan which sporadically enveloped me in a rush of stale air, I could hardly realize that within a few hours darkness might surround me forever. Or I might become a figure so scarred that I would never care to see my family and friends again or be seen. Pictures of my wife and my parents and my brother with their most characteristic expressions appeared momentarily in my imagination as though to emphasize the significance of my thoughts. I wondered with a curious detachment just what death would be like, how it felt, and if one was conscious of dying and what sensations and experiences, if any, would befall after life expired. I remembered dead faces I had seen on Guadalcanal and New Britain, inscrutably fixed in their last living expressions, rendering no clue to the mystery of the Beyond. These thoughts, morbid as they may seem, did not worry me. I regarded them objectively as though I were contemplating the street light at the crossroads in front of my home. They seemed inevitable but separate from the optimism of my feelings. With a burning confidence in living which has never deserted me, I shook them out of my head.

In the wardroom the tables were heaped with steak sandwiches and apples. Percolators, hung in racks by the pass-through to the galley, were spouting steam and the smell of coffee. I began to feel a nervousness in the pit of my stomach, and I was not able to eat the number of steaks I would have liked. I noticed that my officers were eating as lightly. I could feel the tension and attempted to alleviate it with a note of business.

"Be sure that your men put on camouflage paint. Good for the morale. Puts them in the mood."

"It makes 'em look like a bunch of wild Indians," Willis remarked, "if there's nothing on that beach to meet 'em, a lot of them will be damn disappointed, the way they feel now." We laughed.

"We'll be on the Point before the Japs know it," said Estey, "then it'll be easy going from there on."

"If the Navy does its stuff, you're right," said Hanson, and turned to Sellers, "Say Bull, let's go up on deck and see the fireworks."

"It's too dark now," he replied. "All you can see are flashes on the horizon, and you can't hear anything yet. I hope they're really workin' the place over."

There was a momentary silence. Down below I heard the rumbling of our landing craft, amphibian tractors, warming up their engines. They were lined up on the cavernous tank deck just below the maindeck ready to roll over the ramp into the water.

"Come on Ralph, boy! We'll don the war paint. You put on mine and I'll put on yours," exclaimed Willis to Estey, quickly pushing back his chair so that it grated harshly on the brown linoleum deck.

"OK, Will," and after squashing their cigarettes in an ashtray the two disappeared through the passageway.

When I went on deck the dawn was just beginning to break. Overhead, like a gigantic quilt, were thick patches of dark clouds interwoven by strips of gray light. In the east a cold green was sifting through, spreading the daylight and throwing a sheen of silver on the smooth ocean. Slowly that semicircular expanse of new day enlarged until it encompassed the whole sky. There was no sun, no warmth, merely a dull, leaden blanket Peleliu lay off our starboard side, a thin, blue line slightly humped at one end near where Company K was to land. At frequent intervals orange flashes followed by spurts of yellow smoke appeared in the vicinity of the island. Several seconds later I heard the explosions, distant and booming. As we drew nearer we could see the intricate outlines of our ships of war as they lay off the island with their big guns angrily pointed toward it

The flashes came more frequently now, sometimes simultaneously, causing a louder, steadier rumbling which made the deck under my feet tremble. Occasionally from the island rose tremendous jets of flame followed by spiraling columns of black smoke. Where shells struck the water's edge massive clouds of spray burst upwards. The intensity of the bombardment increased as more ships pulled up on the line and opened up with salvo after salvo. The din became a continuous, thundering roar —

Sellers, who was watching the spectacle through his binoculars, turned toward me, his square, rugged face reflecting the fury of the scene, and shouted:

"They're givin' 'em hell. I'd sure hate to be in those bastards' shoes!"

"Goddam right!" I yelled lack. It didn't seem possible that anybody could live under such a shelling.

Below us on the main deck the men had lined the rail, were standing on top of trucks and boxes and craning over each other's shoulders. The crew were at their battle stations, manning the guns, wearing gray helmets and life jackets. The skipper was hanging over the rail of the conn peering through his binoculars and shouting orders to the wheelhouse.

"Right standard rudder!"

With a running of pulleys and the terse commands of a petty officer a guide boat was lowered into the water. The skipper yelled:

"Good Luck!"

The ensign in the boat waved back.

I looked at my watch; six-thirty, time we were preparing to disembark. I signaled to the wheelhouse where the PA system originated, and the speakers blared:

"Now all marines stand by to disembark!"

The men put on their belts and packs and helmets and picked up their weapons. I looked at them for the last time as a company, and I felt very proud. Then the speakers blared again:

"Now all marines lay to your debarkation stations!"

I put on my own gear and climbed down the ladder to my station.

From then on events tumbled one upon the other so rapidly now, as I look back at them, that they flash through my mind in a swift, sometimes disconnected, series of images. Time and space became confused by the incredible violence of battle and actions which were rarely deliberated hot occurred instinctively.

Before I was aware of it I was descending the almost perpendicular ladder from the main deck to the tank deck. When I swung open the heavy steel door I was slapped by the deafening roar of Alligator engines and the blue, swirling exhaust which began to clog my lungs and make my eyes water. I could see the men crawling into the tractor cockpits, through the narrow clearance between the cabs and the overhead. Once I had navigated the difficult climb into the cockpit I looked to see if everyone was with me who should be: First Sergeant Schmittou, my runners, the radio operators, wiremen and Lieutenant Stramel. The exhaust was pouring over us in spite of the great fans which whirred over our heads. Schmittou was turning green from it and looked as though he was about to vomit. Beads of sweat broke out on our faces, and our jackets were already soggy wet and clinging to us. The palms of my hands were hot and slippery. We waited there for what seemed an interminable length of time. Then the tractor ahead raced its engine and began to lumber forward. The bow doors of the ship had separated; the huge ramp had lowered flush with the water. Slowly our tractor ground toward the opening. As it humped over the beginning of the ramp and rumbled down the slope to the water, we were pitched violently forward against the steel plates of the rear of the cab. We leveled off and were churning through the ocean breathing fresh air.

I will never forget the magnitude of the scene that lay around me. The LST's, looking like gigantic fish lolling on the surface of the water, had formed in a ragged line with their gaping snouts facing the island. Hundreds of tractors were pouring out of their bellies, circling, awaiting their turn to form into waves and head for the line of departure which marked the beginning of the final run to the beach. Intermingled with them were snub-nosed landing boats each flying a pennant which signaled the number of the wave that they would lead into the shore, patrol craft acting as markers of critical areas for the execution of the landing, trim gray speedboats carrying officers who bellowed directions through megaphones. Behind the LSTs were the gray transports looming out of the early mist over the tops of the LSTs. Dimly I could see marines, reserve and rear units, scrambling down the cargo nets hung over the sides. The entire flotilla with ships of every conceivable design stretched southward, following the shore line as far as I could see. It seemed to be writhing in scattered confusion with each of these countless ships engaged in her own individual project and many of them steering their own individual courses, skimming in and out with no apparent purpose. But as I watched during brief moments when my own problems did not require my attention, I saw this chaos gradually evolve into a pattern with the smallest craft fitting into a scheme of tremendous proportions.

Momentarily I was stunned by the metallic blasts of the naval salvos. We were rocked by the concussions; our tractor shook in the water; and at times we were so near to the guns that we felt the heat of the flame which belched from the muzzles. The huge warships, appearing angry and menacing, reeled under the recoil of their own fire and seemed to brace themselves for the succeeding salvos. Their massiveness was exaggerated by the pigmy tractors which crawled around them like bugs. I looked toward the beach. It was smothered in black vapor and flying spray and sand. I saw the dive-bombers plunging toward the earth. Flame and smoke shot up when their bombs hit the mark.

Lite all the others, the tractors of our wave were moving around in a circle. The boat flying the numeral pennant 3 swung in front of the lead tractor, the wave commander signaled with his arms, and we veered off in formation toward the beach. Nearing the line of departure I began to see the delineations of the coast. There was the coconut grove, the narrow strip of beach and on the left the Point which was hardly distinguishable from the rest of the shore line and which I thought appeared higher than we had anticipated.

I was startled by swishing sounds followed by a series of thunderous explosions. The rocket ships, converted LCI's, were laying down the last stage of the preparatory bombardment. The staccato roar of thousands of rockets pounding on the beach sounded as though a giant machine gun manned by Hercules had opened up in full fury.

Our turn was next. The driver of my tractor jammed the throttle forward. The machine lurched clumsily, swung toward the beach, and with the tracks churning up a spout of foam on either side, was soon crossing the line.

The sailors on the patrol boats and rocket ships waved and shook their fists as we lunged by and yelled, "Go get 'em, you marines!" I saw my men in the tractors next to mine wave and shout back, but the noise of the engines drowned out their words. We crouched below the gunwale. Our driver closed the port over his head and steered with the periscope. Only the tractor commander, a marine sergeant, was standing up, tall, lean, his broad shoulders bent over the machine gun mounted on the cab in front of him. He wore a leather helmet, and the square mouthpiece of his radio was fixed on his upper lip. I saw his mouth move as he was directing the driver. His voice was hoarse.

"Go left, go left. That's right. No Bill you're too far to the right, keep left Now steady, steady, you're goin' fine. Left more, left That's right, hold it there."

Through the cab door I could see the driver with his head jammed into the matted frame of the periscope. As he was stripped to the waist I could see the muscles in his back strain when he shoved and pulled on the levers. The base of his neck bulged with his exertions, and the veins behind his ears stood out like whipcord. Sweat was streaming down his back, wetting the top of his trousers.

Fixed in a crouched position, my knees were beginning to ache, and I wondered if I would be able to unbuckle them to jump out of the tractor. I looked behind me and saw the men bent over in the same way. They were bracing themselves with their rifle butts stuck underneath them between their legs. Their faces were alert, their eyes in the shadows of their helmets seemed abnormally bright. I believe I winked at Kelly, my blond-headed runner, for he smiled back, I suddenly felt a quizzical amazement at being where I was.

Next to my tractor on the left was Willis with his first platoon. As he told me days later, in his vigorous way, he rigged two shaving mirrors above the level of the cockpit, each facing toward the beach. "With these mirrors I keep the boys in the best of spirits all the way in to the beach," he explained, "and so they all know what's coming off without sticking their heads up. I have someone stationed at each mirror giving us a play by play description just like listening over the radio in Canarsie to a ball game at Ebbets Field."

"And then I have this Polish bey, Dzionkowski, who plays the harmonica, I ask him if he's got his harmonica and he says, 'yes.' So I says to him, 'Give forth, Dzionkowski, and give the boys some cheer with a few polkas.' Pretty soon we're all singing the 'Beer Barrel

Polka,' which helps matters no end and everybody feels much better."

Sergeant Webber, a squad leader in the third platoon, told me something similar.

"We didn't think of using mirrors, but we sure did plenty of singing. The boys were getting a little tense. One kid was sick as a dog and vomited over the side. So Rowe and O'Brien started cracking jokes about Abie the Tailor and singing 'Give My Regards to Broadway.' Just before we hit the beach we were all singing it at the top of our lungs. It sure made us feel good."

I looked at my watch: four minutes until H-Hour, eight-thirty, and the beach was probably six hundred yards away. Seconds went like hours. I pulled back the bolt of my carbine and rammed a round into the chamber. I heard the tank commander again:

"Who's on that radio? Get the hell off, will ye? Yeah, Bill, somebody homing in on the net. They'll probably run me up for cussing. Watch out now, we'll be hitting the reef soon. It's getting shallow. Keep goin' hard, more speed. That's right, steady now. Here's the reef. You're on it now. Jam her into second. Goddammit, put her into second."

The tractor bumped and twisted on the coral. It faltered, choked and stopped, but the engine kept running.

"Goddammit, stick her into second!"

The driver was putting all his weight behind his right arm as he tore down on the lever. The gears stuck for a moment and with a grinding sound followed by a sharp thud rammed into second gear. The tractor, bouncing crazily, rolled on.

"That's the stuff. Go just where I tell you — There're a lot of stakes and obstacles. Left, left, keep left, watch out for that post. That's right, you've passed it now, you're getting near. Now bear right; OK, you're goin' right through 'em — Jesus! that was close. The bastards are firing back!"

I heard the explosion. It was near —

"That's Jap stuff," somebody said.

"You ain't kiddin'."

They were dropping all around us — probably mortars —

I found myself holding my breath and realizing how helpless we were bunched up inside the tractor. What if a mortar shell fell right — Wham! another explosion — too close. My mouth was dry, my lips parched, I was hanging on to the edge of the cab door to prevent myself from tumbling back as the tractor pitched and rolled. The tank commander was bent lower, riding the motions of the machine as though it were a mustang, bellowing his directions.

"You've got sixty yards to go. Look out for those drums on the right, might be mines there. Do ye see 'em? Bear left. Damn, those are bullets! Heads up I'm gonna spray the trees."

The roar of his gun was deafening. I heard the high chatter of Jap machine guns, the thump, thump of heavier stuff. It seemed to come from my left — the Point! Swish, right over our heads — probably forty millimeters — The snapping whine of bullets —

"Son of a bitch," I muttered. "The beach is lousy with the bastards."

"Now, give her the gas. Get over the hump! Steady, steady."

The nose of the tractor shot upward, braced in mid-air; the tracks took hold, and we leveled off and jerked to a halt. Shattered coconut trees and tall splintered stumps loomed over us. The tank commander nodded his head, and I gave the order to pile out. I saw the beach come to meet me as I rolled over the side. The impact of the eight-foot jump jarred my legs and momentarily upset my balance. Regaining it, I raced across the beach.

PART THREE: AFTER LANDING

CHAPTER FIVE

AFTER running as hard as I could for about seventy-five yards I slid into a shell hole out of breath, my lips and tongue as dry as sandpaper. Black vapor and the pungent odor of gunpowder which was seeping from the earth helped to clog my throat. Sweat was running off the end of my nose. I rolled a swig of water around in my mouth. Looking behind I saw that Kelly and Blackburn, my runners, and the radio operator and Stramel were in the hole with me. Schmittou was just over the edge of the hole flattened behind a bush. A bullet snapped into the dirt right next to me. I heard vicious rattlings of shots and earth-shaking bursts of mortar shells which fell in a relentless pattern, closer and closer, to the right, to the left, straddling our position. Shrapnel whistled and plunked into the trees.

I could not see my platoons, but I thought I heard the sound of their firing on my right and left.

"Corpsman up here!" Schmittou was calling, "Burton's hit." Delbarter, big, muscular, crawled out of the hole.

"Hello, control, this is five; hello, control, this is five. Do you hear me? Over." That was the radio; Sellers calling. He should be about fifty yards down the beach.

"Send up stretchers. We're getting casualties," I told him.

"Comin' right up," his drawl blurred over the air.

I was trying to get in with my platoons on the radio; I had to know how they were doing. "Hello one, hello two, hello three: This is control. Do you hear me? Over," the radio operator droned on. No word.

Colonel Ross from Regiment jumped into the hole. Good God! What was he doing here? He must have landed too far to the left.

"What outfit is this?"

"K Company. Like a cigarette?" I offered him one.

"No thanks. I've got to be moving. Take care of my radio operator; he's been hit."

"No, he's dead, Colonel," said Delbarter.

"Oh," he paused: "Good Luck." He scrambled out of the hole.

I heard a scuffling behind me. Blackburn was wounded in the arm. His young face turned very white, and his lips curled up with the pain. I got Sellers on the radio again.

"Where in hell are the stretchers?"

"I sent 'em up fifteen minutes ago. They should be there by now. There's Japs all around us back here."

A few minutes later Dempsey and Hooker appeared with a stretcher. They laid Burton on it and carried him off. A mortar shell struck just then, very near. I saw Dempsey standing up, raising a hand which was dripping with blood. He pointed to his fingers.

"Two of 'em gone," he shouted, and damned if he wasn't smiling!

The radio operator was still calling the platoons. Still no answer. The uncertainty became agonizing. I heard the heavy throbbing of big stuff, the unmistakable persistence of Jap machine guns from the vicinity of the Point I saw flame and smoke rising from our beach, heard the sizzling of burning Alligators, and the mortars were pounding about us with more intensity. The Jap fire was building up.

Suddenly I heard the call I had been waiting for. It came slurred and crackling at first, then clear as a bell.

"Hello, control, this is one, hello, control, this is one, do you hear me? Over."

"Yeah, Willis, I hear you, what's the dope?"

"Hello, old man, I'm up just behind the third platoon. Estey and Koval were hit. They've had a hell of a lot of casualties and need stretcher bearers badly. I'm seein' what I can do up here."

"Do you have contact with the second on your right?"

"No, nothing in there but Japs."

"Well, push through and take the Point," I told him. "I'm coming right up."

"OK, OK," he answered, "that's what I figured."

I called Major McNulty at Battalion on the radio. "We're pretty well shot up and there's a gap between my two assault platoons. I'm throwing the first platoon in to take the Point. The goddam naval gunfire didn't faze the Japs! We need stretcher bearers!"

"All right, Bub, I'll have L Company fill in the gap. I'll send up everybody I can spare with stretchers."

But there was still no word from the second platoon.

Kelly, whom I had sent up to find Estey and the third platoon, returned with a bullet hole through his shin. Pantingly he told me:

"Jese, there are K Company guys dead and wounded lyin' all around. Mr. Estey got it twice in the arm. He's layin' in a hole and looks pretty bad. They're askin' for you. They got shot up when they were goin' up the beach toward that Point Yeah, and they think Koval's dead, and McNeel, and Webber took over. I got hit up here about ten yards." Just then a bullet clipped off the radio antenna.

The decision was made now; I had committed my whole company.

I told the radioman to follow me, rolled out of the hole and, running from tree to tree, headed toward the Point.

The human wreckage I saw was a grim and tragic sight. First it was bewildering; then it made me hot with anger; but finally my feelings cooled to accepting a gruesome inevitable fact There was Gasser, whose face, always pale, was as white as the sand on which he lay. Shrapnel had shattered his rifle and a piece had penetrated his neck. It was an effort for him to grin, but he did. I saw Culjak, very tall and dark, with a Bloody bandage around his arm. Kneeling in a hole in the sand I asked him what had happened to him. He was in the second platoon.

"I was on the left with Bandy and Dolan trying to keep contact with the third platoon. But I got separated from my outfit. I don't know what happened to them. Then I ran into a Jap and killed him with a grenade, but he got me in the arm."

I saw McMatt lying on his side with a small hole in his stomach which oozed purple blood. Someone had taken off his clothes. Slowly he turned his head toward me, and I saw that his blue eyes were glassy. He opened his mouth, and his white lips formed a word, but no sound came forth. Exhausted by the effort he let his head slump back, and blood was drooling from his mouth. The corpsman who was squatting next to him shook his head.

These were only three of the wounded and dying which littered the edge of the coconut grove from where we had landed to the Point. As I ran up the beach I saw them lying nearly shoulder to shoulder; some of them mine; others from outfits which landed immediately behind us. I saw a ghastly mixture of bandages, bloody and mutilated skin;

men gritting their teeth, resigned to their wounds; men groaning and writhing in their agonies; men outstretched or twisted or grotesquely transfixed in the attitudes of death; men with their entrails exposed or whole chunks of body ripped out of them. There was Graham, snuffed out a hero, lying with four dead Japs around him; and Windsor, flat on his face, with his head riddled by bullets and his arms pointed toward a pillbox where five Japs slumped over a machine gun; and Sharp, curled up on his side, still holding his automatic rifle which pointed to a huddle of dead Japs thirty yards away. His aim had been good. Stieferman was alive, his face and body peppered by shrapnel. His words came slowly and raspingly.

"Hello, Captain. Sorry I had to get it like this, but I saw those three Japs, and as soon as I threw a grenade at 'em I got one in return. It cut me up a little bit, but I got all three of them. I know I did."

I saw McNeel, his eyes turned up in death, a yellow pallor on his rugged face. He was lying directly in front of a forty millimeter gun lodged in a pillbox of reinforced concrete. The gun was scarred and wrenched from its base. Inside dead Japs sprawled on top of each other. An open, half-empty canteen and a Tommy gun by next to McNeel's head.

No wonder the Japs had done such damage. The Point, rising thirty feet above the water's edge, was of solid, jagged coral, a rocky mass of sharp pinnacles, deep crevasses, tremendous boulders. Pillboxes, reinforced with steel and concrete, had been dug or blasted in the base of the perpendicular drop to the beach. Others, with coral and concrete piled six feet on top were constructed above, and spider holes were blasted around them for protecting infantry. It surpassed by far anything we had conceived of when we studied the aerial photographs.

Willis had moved swiftly and had already assaulted the Point; the sound of sporadic firing came from the ether side. Jap dead fringed the base of the rise to the Point and filled up the niches and holes in the coral. They were big healthy men, and had new equipment. I climbed up the rocks and saw Willis' muscular, bowlegged figure.

"Good going, Will," I congratulated him, "you've done a wonderful job."

"It wasn't me, it was these men," he answered waving his arm in a wide sweeping gesture.

"We've got to hold this place now," I said, "how many men do you have left?"

"About thirty, all that's left of my platoon and Estey's. What happened to the second? There's nobody on our right."

"I don't know," I answered, "I think they've had a hell of a rough time. It looks like we're isolated up here."

The men were in a line behind boulders forming a circular, all-around defense of the Point. They were resting, occasionally rising up to shoot at a stray Jap. Otherwise it was quiet, except for the steady thumping of mortar shells on the beach and the reef behind us, and the distant chattering of machine guns far off to our right. The immediate silence seemed ominous. Standing on the rocks I looked back and could see gray files of troops moving inland from the beach, through the debris of the coconut grove. They would push on the right and overrun the airfield. I wondered how the fight was progressing over there, but there was no way of knowing now. The entire beach was swarming with tractors, men evacuating wounded and unloading supplies, aid stations which had been hurriedly set up to meet the sudden rush of casualties. The sands were black with milling men.

"What a target!" I exclaimed to Willis, "No wonder the Japs are raising so much hell!"

One evening as we were sitting around my tent back in our base camp wishing we had some bottles of cold beer, Willis described to me some of the things which happened to his platoon when he assaulted the Point. As he talked, his sunburned face, wide and prominent across the forehead and cheekbones, narrowing abruptly to a thin, tight-lipped mouth and a jutting chin, frequently broke into a grin that twisted the entire right side of his face upward. He spoke with the vigor and razor-edged accent of a downtown New Yorker, continually throwing his right arm out stiffly in front of him in broad, emphatic gestures.

"When I landed, the first thing I thought was: It's all fooled up. I've got to keep my platoon together. I ran into Estey in a shell hole, and he had been shot in the arm and was bleeding pretty badly. After I talked to you over the radio we shoved off to the Point. Estey had smashed most of the protecting Jap infantry, and before I knew it we were swarming all over their pillboxes and chasing them over the rocks.

"This boy King had a close shave. He was pulling off a one-man attack on a pillbox, crawling and throwing grenades at the embrasure. The Japs opened up on him, and a bullet zipped right through his helmet. If his head had been made with a bump on it he'd have been a dead man. But he kept going. Then another bullet smacked his cartridge belt and caromed off. Still King didn't stop, and, wriggling behind a big rock, he jumped up quickly, threw a grenade and ducked down. It exploded in the embrasure, a perfect heave, and silenced the pillbox and the Japs inside of it for good. When we reached the top of the Point the Japs were running away across the open rocky stretch on the other side. My boys lined up as though they were in a shooting gallery at Coney Island and proceeded to pick them off with ease! I remember one Jap who left a trail of smoke behind him, his pack evidently on fire. He was screaming like a frightened monkey. Then he fell down, still burning tip, and didn't move after that.

"We knew that there was a large pillbox with a forty-millimeter gun just to our left at the foot of the cliff. We kept an eye on it to see that none of the Japs inside trial to get out and turned our attention to the shooting gallery. When that was finished I sat down on a rock, lit a cigarette and tried to figure the best way to knock out this pillbox which was hard to get at because of the big rocks which stuck out over it. I heard the bastards inside jabbering, and that made me mad. I figured out a plan. A squad covered the rear exit of the pillbox. Anderson, one of my corporals, sneaked part way down the rocks about twenty yards in front of the embrasure, while I crawled to a cut in the cliff where I could heave a grenade without being shot at. I threw a smoke grenade just in front of the embrasure so that the Japs could not see what we were doing. I ran over to Anderson who was about to aim a rifle grenade at the embrasure. Suddenly the forty millimeter opened up at rapid fire and rattled our composure to say the least. Balls of flame swished over our heads. For a moment it looked as though the Jap had spotted us and were trying to drill the rock in front of us. I thought my time was up. But luckily the gun stopped firing as suddenly as it had started. Anderson squinted down his sights and pulled the trigger. The grenade launched perfectly and smacked the gun on the barrel. It ignited something inflammable, and after a big explosion the pillbox burst into flame, and black smoke poured out of the embrasure and the exit. I heard the Japs screaming and their ammunition spitting and snapping as the heat exploded it. Three Japs, with bullets popping in their belts and flames clinging to their legs, raced from the exit waving their arms and letting out yells of pain. The squad I had placed there finished them off.

"Anderson was all over the place. Just before we knocked out that pillbox at the base of the cliff he accounted for another one singlehanded. As he was dodging and jumping from rock to rock I saw him suddenly twist sideways almost in mid-air. I thought he was hit. But a bullet had only shot off his canteen. Moving faster he jumped over the Jap line of fire and hit the deck on the flank of the pillbox. There he was momentarily hidden from my view by some rocks, but then I saw him jump again — this time right on top of the pillbox. As calmly as though he was pitching horseshoes he tossed a phosphorus grenade into the air vent I saw a puff of smoke. The machine gun in the pillbox stopped firing, and Anderson, appearing very unconcerned, jumped down among the boulders and ran on to the top of the Point."

Willis ceased his narrative. There was a lull in the conversation. Over in the camp area I heard voices singing "For Me and My Gal." Some of the men who are slated to go home, I thought.

"May I come in, Captain?" Somebody was standing outside the front of the tent.

"Certainly, come in," I answered.

Sergeant Jarvi loomed into the dim, oil light. He was a tremendous man, broad of shoulder, and stood as straight as a ramrod. His face was wide, with prominent jowls and cold blue eyes. He wore a great handle-bar mustache which nearly equaled the width of his face. The ends, curled into sharp points, quivered when he talked. He should have been dressed in a Polish grenadier's uniform of a century ago. His voice had a tough, slightly accented edge.

"I understand you're writin' a book on this last blitz," he said.

"Yes, I've just started it," I replied.

"Do you think it will be published?"

"I hope so," I said, a little startled, "but that depends on a lot of other people."

"Well, anyway, Captain," he began, and I thought I saw a glint in his eyes. "I wish you would put the people back home straight on this matter of souvenirs. They all think that unless you come back with a sword or a set of Jap teeth you ain't seen any action. But you know, Captain, most of the time the front line troops never get any souvenirs. We kill the damn Japs and then have to keep goin' to kill some more. We don't have the time to pick up any souvenirs. Then these yardbirds from the rear come up after a couple of days when it's safe and get all the gravy, without even bein' shot at!"

"You're perfectly right, Jarvi," I answered, laughing, "I'll put that in the book. In fact I'll quote you word for word."

It was ten-thirty. I called Major McNulty on the radio and told him that the Point was secured.

"That's fine," he answered, "what supplies do you need?"

"We need water, grenades, ammunition and barbed wire, and as many reinforcements as you can scrape together. I've only got about thirty men up here. We must have

51

machine guns! Mine were nearly all shot up when they landed."

"Ok, Bub," he answered, "I'll get the stuff up to you as soon as I can by tractor along the reef. Be on the lookout for L Company moving into the gap on the right. They will make contact with you."

There was nothing to do but wait, rest and strengthen our line. The men had already started to build foxholes of rocks and fallen logs. The clouds had broken overhead, and the sun was relentlessly beating down on us, reflecting from the coral rocks with doubled intensity. As the men worked the sweat drenched their clothes and skin. In the bay the warships were firing far inland, and even where we were we could feel the concussion. The Point seemed almost unscarred by the terrific bombardment we had seen before the landing. I was amazed that the pillboxes had weathered it untouched. Few trees had grown in the coral, and what ones ware there ware short and crooked and gnarled. Our shelling had reduced most of them to jagged stumps. We had paid clearly for the Point, but there was compensation in the fact that we had counted no dead Japs and that we now held a very strategic position. There was no possible way of knowing how many out of my entire company had been killed or wounded. I knew there were a lot, nearly two-thirds I estimated, figuring that the second platoon over on the right had suffered as heavily as the first and third. Stramel radioed that most of my machine-gun platoon had been mowed down on the beach and there were no more than eight men left and all the guns had been knocked out. Hanson radioed me that the mortar section was still intact down the beach where Sellers was, but there was no wire communication available to the Point. We would have to rely on the radio to direct mortar fire, but the batteries were fading fast and would probably be entirely dead by nightfall. Sellers was dangerously straddled by Jap mortars.

I walked along the line and met Webber and Hahn. What was left of their third platoon was in position on the line, and the three of us had time to sit down on the baked rocks for a few minutes and have a sweaty cigarette. We were dripping with perspiration, and our wet fingers soaked and spoiled our smokes before we really had time to enjoy them. They were anxious to talk about the fight Hahn's gray eyes were bright with excitement, and a half grin crooked the thin line of his mouth. He pointed to a rise in the coral behind me. "Right there," he said, "Humplik and I walked right into three Japs who were setting up a heavy machine gun. We came barging around these big boulders like two damn fools and were on top of them before we knew it. They looked up at us and started jabbering excitedly and reaching for hand grenades. Luckily I had one in my hand which I threw just in time. It went off in the middle of them and killed two. The other one took off at a dead run after tossing a grenade at us, and Humplik drilled him. The grenade hit directly between us. It was a dud. We set the Jap gun on the line, up there by those high rocks."

"I saw it," I said, "have you got plenty of ammunition for it?"

"Sure, there's stacks of it in some of these pillboxes."

Jap mortars began to drop shells on the beach, close to our lines. We ducked behind the rocks and wailed for them to pound in our positions. But fortunately they stopped just below the Point and started back down the shore line in a rapid series of explosions.

"God!" exclaimed Webber, "that's murder for all those people crowded together on that beach!"

"Yeah," added Hahn, "and they could certainly raise hell with us if they dropped a concentration in here."

"You know, Captain," said Webber changing the subject, "I wonder what the Japs thought when we hit the beach. We were all striped up with camouflage paint and poured out of the tractors hollering like a bunch of Indians and charging at the Japs full speed. Several guys were shouting 'Gung Ho!' but most of them had their own war cry. We ran smack into the Japs as they were running out of their pillboxes to their spider holes."

"Damn right," I said, "if you hadn't moved in so fast we would never have had the momentum to take this Point." Webber flicked away his cigarette and leaned forward with his elbows on his knees. He was as unruffled as though he were riding in a streetcar. "And you should have seen Rowe," he went on, grinning broadly, showing straight teeth. "He has these white workman's gloves, and every once in a while as he moved up with his BAR under his arm, which is almost as big as he is, he would stop right in the middle of all the shooting, pull off his gloves, take a nail file from his pocket and file his nails. Then he would twirl his mustache. And Lindsey Jones was just as funny. When the Japs were all around us below the Point, Lindsey sat in a bush picking them off, sayin' all the time in his southern accent, 'Mah, mah, theah suah a' lot of Japs around heah.'"

"The Japs didn't seem to bother him much," commented Hahn, smiling. Sweat rolling down Hahn's face left streaks in the camouflage paint and the gray coral dirt smudged across the top of his cheeks. He took off his helmet and rubbed the perspiration from the back of his neck.

"Nothing can bother that guy," replied Webber, "he's as rugged as an ox. When Carter was hit, Lindsey went over to help him. He was putting a bandage on Carter's chest when he saw a Jap sneakin' up on him. He waved his arm at the Jap and yelled at him, 'Git away from heah, you Jap, can't you see I'm fixin' a man?' The Jap got behind a tree and all Lindsey could see of him was the edge of his helmet sticking out on either side of the tree. So Lindsey put aside the bandage, took up his BAR and fired a shot which went right through the tree and into the Jap's head."

I told Hahn and Webber what I knew of our situation and to keep a sharp lookout for L Company which was to close the gap on our right, then continued along the line which in total length could not have been over a hundred yards. I saw Sovik, Willis' platoon sergeant, who told me about a Jap who wanted to surrender and come into our lines just after we had seized the Point. His words tumbled out quickly.

"The Jap had his pack on and was carrying his weapon, so we shot him, just to be on the safe side, and damned if he didn't blow up. He must have been loaded down with dynamite and grenades."

"Yeah," drawled Lees, who had come up while Sovik was talking and whose sallow, hardened face bore a casual expression, "they're tricky little bastards. You've got to watch 'em. There are lots of 'em running around out there with our helmets on."

The men were asking for water; their canteens were dry. There were only a few grenades left and what ammunition each man had in his belt. We looked expectantly toward the beach for the Alligator which would bring us supplies, and to our right for signs of L Company moving up.

I was sitting behind a white boulder trying to enjoy a cigarette. I felt as though I was in an oven, and the rocks were hot to the touch. My thoughts wandered to the dead men lying on the slope of the Point. So many lives had been snuffed out so quickly that it seemed impossible and incredible. Once again I thought of a fantastic dream with no logic, only a pattern of grotesque, lugubrious shapes and a background of tuneless music and uncontrolled rhythms.

The explosion of a mortar shell startled me —Then more — they were dropping in our midst. Shrapnel whined through the rocks, ricocheting and clipping the tree stumps. I heard a voice say very calmly, "Looks like I'm hit." A chunk of steel smashed into the rocks on my left throwing chips of stone. Again the voice, "Yes, I'm hit all right; in the leg. Feels like the bone's broken." The barrage stopped. There was silence, and I waited for the cry "Corpsman!" None came. One more round fell on the edge of the cliff, I looked around; yes, it was Duncan who was wounded in the leg, and he was as cool as ice. His face had turned as gray as the rocks around him. They carried him to the water's edge to wait for the tractor. If the Japs continued those concentrations soon there would be none of us left. But perhaps they did not know —

Then I saw Sergeant Bandy of the second platoon scrambling over the rocks toward me. He had lost contact in the area of the gap and had just found our positions. I was certainly glad to see him. "What happened to the second platoon?" I asked him. He waited until he got his breath back before answering, and he wiped the sweat out of his eyes with the sleeve of his jacket. About a hundred and fifty yards in from the beach most of the second platoon had been caught in a tank trap and on trying to assault out of it had been terribly shot up. The trap was nearly fifteen yards wide, ten feet deep and extended parallel to the shore line for several hundred yards. It was a mammoth trench with sloping sides of loose coral sand, hidden in the torn and uprooted underbrush of the coconut grove. It was raked by machine guns from the sides and from the precipitous coral ridge to its front where pillboxes had been blasted in the rock. Woodyard was dead and Macek, his platoon sergeant, had been hit in the arm as soon as they had landed. Good God! I called Sellers on the radio and told him the information.

"We just got the same word down here," he said. "We're going to try to evacuate what's left of the second platoon as soon as we can. Battalion is bringing up tanks."

Dusk was approaching fast. The tractor with the supplies had just arrived, and we had to work quickly unloading it so that it could get back to the beach before night. Case after case of hand grenades and ammunition, cans of water which tasted of oil and had grown hot under the sun, rolls of barbed wire, crates of "C" rations, we piled on the coral ledge at the foot of the cliff and by chain gang lugged it up the rocks to the top of the rise where it was distributed to the men. The crew of the tractor gave us two of their machine guns which strengthened our scanty line considerably. Parties moved out in front of the positions to lay the barbed wire. Snipers harassed them, and a bullet lodged in the heart of a redheaded lid with freckles who had just been talking to me. "Gosh, Captain," he had said, "I never expected it to be as rough as this. If I live through it, I sure hope I never see another one like it." He had walked away with a broad smile on his grimy face. The tractor left and rolled down the reef. Mortar shells began to drop near it, following it all the way back but miraculously never scoring a hit.

Sniper fire had increased, popping from every direction outside of our perimeter. Occasionally a mortar shell would burst dangerously near. Two squads of L Company's machine-gun platoon had worked their way up to us during the afternoon, but no troops had appeared on our right where the gap was. Haggerty with his eighty-one millimeter mortar observation group had joined us, but he had no communication with his guns two thousand yards behind us. So he and his four men reinforced our line, manning a machine gun. Over his carrot-red hair he was wearing a blue baseball cap.

My radio was on its last legs. I had heard Sellers say that they had successfully evacuated what was left of the second platoon from the tank trap under the cover of tanks and that an estimated 150 Japs had moved in the gap. Then the radio faded out I called him loudly for more information, but there was no answer.

It was almost dark. I was talking over our situation with Willis when Monk Meyer and Dolan appeared over the edge of the cliff from battalion headquarters. They had stolen through the coconut grove behind us and said it was lousy with Japs. Battalion had established a provisional line about two hundred yards had after the second platoon had been withdrawn from the tank trap.

"You're isolated up here," he said, looking at me, "and surrounded by Japanese."

"Yes, I know that," I replied, "Nobody has made contact with us."

"A Company and L Company have been trying to all afternoon. They had the hell shot out of 'em attempting to move into the gap which must be over two hundred yards wide," he said; then after a pause: "Do you think you can hold out?"

"Sure we can. Looks like we'll have to."

'Well I must get going now. I think I'll swim back outside the reef. Take it easy and good luck." He disappeared over the rocks, and we sat silently for a few moments absorbing his information. I heard the water lapping against the rocks at the foot of the cliff. The evening was quiet and breathless.

"Anyway," said Willis, suddenly, "there's one thing to be said for our situation. We'll be able to kill some more of the bastards!"

Considering that first bloody day I often wonder how we survived it as well as we did. The naval gun-fire had little effect on the hard coral ridges which commanded our beach and on the Japs who had dug into them with the laborious persistency of moles. Extending from the Point inland and then running parallel to the beach was a coral ridge about twenty-five feet high. From this as well as from the Point the Japanese raked the beach and the flat area of the coconut grove with murderous machine-gun, rifle and mortar fire. In spite of these odds, the men moved into this hell with a furious momentum. On our left, by the use of two platoons, that momentum carried us over the Point. On the right, the momentum died when the second platoon was caught in the tank trap which was covered by that ridge about fifty yards in front of them. But there was only one platoon, and the odds were hopelessly against them. A few of the second attained the ridge, but the Japs, lodged there in great numbers, cut them down with bullets and grenades and drove the rest into the tank trap.

Wiginton is a private first class and a member of the second platoon. He could not be over eighteen; he is very small and exceedingly proud of his size. Nevertheless he is a man and a big one. He comes from Alabama and is also exceedingly proud of that. One evening, two weeks after we had returned from Peleliu to our base camp, I asked him over to my tent to tell me his version of what happened to the second platoon.

"I can't tell you very much about it, sir," he said, "but I can tell you what I know."

I offered him a cigar and was surprised that he refused it.

"It was like this," he started. "Just after we landed on the beach, the fellas began gettin' shot by machine guns from that ridge. Then after a lot of runnin' with bullets and shrapnel flyin' all over, I found myself in this deep tank trap, and already I could see that everybody was split up and separated, and guys with blood on 'em were all over the tank trap. Any time anybody tried to climb out and keep attacking they was shot I didn't see him but someone told me that Lootenant Woodyard had been killed by a bullet through the head, and Sergeant Macek wounded. So where I was nobody was in charge. We was all terribly pooped out from runnin' on that sandy coral and tryin' to climb on it out of the tank trap. I just couldn't get enough water, and Susinka was vomitin'. Jenkins, the corpsman, was a real hero. He not only patched all the boys up but he went out over the tank trap to pull the wounded 'uns in. We couldn't get any stretchers to carry 'em back, which we couldn't a done anyway because the Japs was infiltratin' from that ridge all around the trap. So they just lay there, some of 'em groanin', some of 'em pretty quiet. There was one guy layin' there from another outfit with a little hole in his arm who gave me a pain in the neck. He was whinin' and carryin' on and sayin', 'What are they gonna do, leave us here to die? Get some stretchers and get us out of here.' I told him to shut up mighty quick, 'cause Schleyer was there too with a nasty hole through his loins not sayin' a word. Daily's squad was near caught between the ridge and the trap. He was tryin' to get 'em back into the trap 'cause they could do nothin' up there but get killed.

"I seen Thompson up behind a bush with bis rifle over his knees, lookin' around just as cool as a cucumber sayin' all the time, I'll get those little bastards.' Then suddenly a mortar shell landed right in the trap ten feet from where we were. I gulped a couple-a times and thought I was goin' to my Maker. A big column of blue smoke spouted up, but the shell didn't go off. We sure were a scared bunch a guys then.

"When Luciak crawled out of the trap to try to get back to the CP to get help and got killed, I sure felt awful bad. Old 'Pop,' ye know, one a the nicest guys I ever knew. Meantime the Jap mortars was droppin' all around us and the bullets started to hit right in the tank trap.

"I seen Jack Henry comin' down along the tank trap with one hand danglin' by a piece of skin and the other one riddled awful bad, all covered with blood. Jenkins, who was takin' a look at Pop, seen him too and fixed him up right away. He saved Jack's life, you know; he'd a died sure from bleedin'. I hear that the docs aboard ship fixed up his hands, and he'll be able to use 'em again. Meantime the boys were startin' to make their farewell speeches and all that. We was figurin' we'd never get out of there and that we'd all get it sooner or later.

"Then I found a radio and got holda Lootenant Stramel in the CP and gave him all the dope about what was happenin' here. I seen Jack LaBerge, and he was goin' strong even if he did have three pieces of shrapnel in his back. They told me he just shot some Japs up at the end of the tank trap. His machine guns had teen firin' and doin' a lot of damage to the Japs up on the ridge. The Japs tried for a long time to locate them with mortars. But I don't think they ever did. Finally towards evenin' some stretcher bearers came along the trap, and tanks came up firin' hard at the Japs. Then Lootenant Stramel gave us orders to withdraw. The Japs had mostly stopped shootin' as it was getting' pretty dark, except for one machine gun right up in front of us. So this little redheaded kid, Gatto, jumped outa the trap and started throwin' grenades and shootin' his rifle at the gun, and kept it busy while we got the wounded outa the trap. I hollered at Gatto to come back but he didn't hear me. So I climbed outa the trap to take a look and saw that he was dead, shot up awful bad. That boy sure died a hero.

"Then with the tanks protectin' us we all got outa the trap and ran back to the lines Battalion had set up. There couldn't have been more than eight or nine of us left, and when I saw the guys of K Company there at the CP I really felt glad, I guess I was sort of cryin' to myself."

The movies were on that night at the theater, and I didn't want to keep Wiggie any longer, so we said good night, and he left.

The next evening Sergeant LaBerge arrived from the hospital. He was thin, and his high cheekbones stood out prominently in the dim light in my tent. His eyes were black as night and caught a pin-point reflection of the feeble bulb which hung over my table. He was the leader of the machine-gun section which went over to help the second platoon. He was a little sky about telling his story, but after I drew him out with a few questions he started off: "The first thing happened before we landed. The rear of our tractor was shot off, probably by a mortar."

"Did it hurt anybody?" I asked.

"No it didn't. The tractor began filling up with water, but it made the beach all right When we piled out bullets were peppering against the side of the tractor. I don't know why, but nobody was hit.

"When I got over to the tank trap I saw that everything was fouled up; wounded and dying all around, and the Japs had lines of fire right over our heads. Jack Henry stuck his helmet on a stick and raised it above the level of the trap. A bullet went right through it. I found a position for McKinstry to set up his gun, just over the edge of the trap in a Jap trench about five feet away. It was risky, but it was risky just bein' alive."

"Yes," I said, "McKinstry told me about that. He fired thirteen hundred rounds from there and mowed down a platoon of Japs who were trying to encircle the tank trap. Whaley was on the gun and was shot in the heel, then Inman was shot and finally McKinstry got it in the neck."

"That's right, Mick fell over as though he were dead. I dragged him into the trap and bandaged him up and got his gun. I can't remember when each of my men were hit, but they were dropping fast. I had the ones who were left strip down the guns. They were full of sand and had jammed. Then I got word from Mr. Stramel that you wanted us up on the Point. So with Henry and myself in the lead we took off down the tank trap toward the Point. I came to a sharp bend, and suddenly about twenty-five Japs ran across the trap and up the other side. We looked at them and they looked at us. Henry cut loose with his Tommy gun and I remember pulling the trigger of my old M-1 as fast as I could. We killed six of 'em. The others started throwin' hand grenades from the top of the trap. I felt a sharp, stinging pain in my back. I got mad as hell! I had seen Mike Pollinger shot dead between the eyes, many others wounded all over their bodies, and a mortar had just cut up five more of my men. And the Japs were wearing clean khaki; some of them had green nets over their helmets; they hadn't even worked up a sweat. I bellowed at the boys to set up the guns. They were sort of stunned, I guess, they just stood there looking dumb. 'Set up those f— guns!' I hollered again, and they went to work. But the sand kicked up by the mortars had worked into the mechanisms again. The damn things jammed. Then Henry's hands were nearly shot off by a machine-gun burst. They looked awful, and I sent him back down the trap. I looked up quickly and saw the Japs over the edge of the trap running along in a file. They were movin' away from us toward you fellas on the Point. Suddenly everything was quiet.

"It was getting late so we moved back to where some of the second platoon were, carrying our wounded with us. Then the tanks arrived, and we withdrew to the beach without even being shot at."

I offered him a cigarette which he refused; then I lit my own. LaBerge was gazing down at the dirt floor. He crossed one knee over the other.

"By the way, Captain," he said looking up, "have you heard about Whaley and Sutherland?"

I shook my head.

"They got into an argument about something on the LST. They concluded that the first one to turn back after he was wounded was yellow. That's why Whaley refused to go to the rear until he was hit for the fourth time; two bullet wounds and two shrapnel wounds. He was too weak to go on after the last one."

CHAPTER SIX

As BLACKNESS crept up and completely enveloped us, we were subdued to an eery silence. Even the clicking sounds of a small stone falling from the rough surface of a rock, probably brushed off by the sweep of a man's elbow, seemed a harsh disturbance. Though there was no moon, the sky, massed by thick and voluminous clouds, was just light enough to reveal the weird and grotesque silhouettes of knotted trees and stumps. The jagged, pinnacled rocks rose like witches' fingers, and the bald, cracked humps of boulders, appearing indiscriminately and catching the merest reflection of light, seemed like tremendous human pates which had been brutally clubbed to submissiveness. Surrounding us were the woods which had become dark and impenetrable in the night.

When one lies in a hole peering intently into the black, listening, smelling, hearing only the sound of one's breathing, waiting, expecting, the stillness may become appalling, dead objects may rise slowly and live, the motionless may move, sounds of leaves stirred by the breeze may become the sneaking movements of human feet, a friend may be an enemy, an enemy a friend, until, unless controlled by toughness of mind, one's imagination may become haunted by the unseen and the unheard. One may panic under this strain, jump up, screaming hoarsely and firing his weapon blindly all around him until shot dead by his friends because he is endangering their lives and might have already shot one of them. One may suddenly see incredible sights in the trees such as a shining yellow airplane, hung there, swarming with Japs and belching fire and bullets, and whisper what he sees to his buddy who then gets a friend and carries the raving one off the line. Another may be merely nervous and fire shots at nothing giving away his position to Japanese scouts who are silently watching from the underbrush. Still another, feeling no alertness and allowing himself to be overcome with fatigue and being a slouch of a man, may fall asleep and meet a dreadful end on the point of an enemy bayonet. That man betrays himself as well as his friends.

The Jap loves the night, and he loves to sneak. He is an animal who prowls noiselessly with padded, two-toed shoes on his feet. When he attacks by himself or with a few others and suddenly appears out of the night over our holes with bayonet and knife, he is dangerous and clever. But like all animals he succumbs easily to the instinct of the mass, and when he attacks in great numbers he is blind and stupid and, like a wolf, seeks a crowd and the protection of numbers. Then he is easy prey for our weapons.

The Jap is treacherous and unscrupulous and thinks nothing of his own life. Perhaps he is fanatic; perhaps he is merely stupid in underestimating us. When he screams "Banzai!" it is to convince himself of his own spirit. If it is to undermine our spirit, it is a pathetic endeavor. When he defends he is tenacious and brave and shoots well until we have disorganized his positions which are so heavily constructed and thoroughly dug in that it is often very costly to smash them. Then, confused and leaderless, he huddles in his pillbox or cave attempting to kill as many of us as he can before his death. If the terrain favors him, for a while he will succeed in doing so, but his defeat and death are inevitable.

I wanted to catch some sleep during the early hours of darkness as the Japs would probably attack later on. I lay down on the ground which was strewn with stones and stiff, prickling growth and found myself wedged between two rocks. I raised up and tried to rake the stones out from under me with my fingers but found that most of them were firmly embedded. In spite of the fact that I was extremely tired, the immediate concern of trying to twist my body into a position which would ease the prodding of the stones kept me awake. Alternately, each of my legs would go to sleep requiring a painful shift to wake them up, and periodically the small of my right foot would develop a cramp. My body finally became used to these discomforts, and I was able to lie still, drifting into that drowsy state of mind when thoughts of the past flow swiftly and easily.

Landing on the beach, the attack on the Point, the noise and the grime and the blood and the agonies and the heroisms of battle, all seemed lost in the passage of time, as though I had seen them sometime in my life bat not today. As though time had turned itself backwards, I thought of much older and more vivid memories: when I was twelve and used to walk to school every morning with a green lunch box under my arm and on returning in the afternoon, used to squash with my feet the tar blisters on the hot, asphalt road; or read the funny-papers on the parlor rug; or wait for the sound of my father's Dodge as it ground into second gear to climb the grade of the driveway — or in the evening sit in my mother's rocking chair in her room watching the flies and moths attracted by the light beat themselves against the window screen — or mow the long green stretch of lawn which was guarded on either side by weeping willows and terraced in the back by my father's flower gardens; or dean the bird bath of droppings and fill it with fresh water; or lie in the hammock on the gray-floored porch and read G. A. Henty or Alexander Dumas and smell the honeysuckle and the roses and hollyhocks which bunched on the white railing, or clip the hedge and edge the rich earth at its base until I was dripping with perspiration and felt that I had done a good day's work; or paint the cellar doors a dark green and rub off what paint had smeared on my fingers with turpentine which I always found in a greasy bottle on the garage tool shelf, I thought of boarding school in the farmland along the Delaware, of the plowed fields stretching over the rolling hills, of the brown-paneled classrooms which smelled of chalk and the vibrant expressions of the stocky, large-headed teacher who stood by the blackboard and threw a piece of chalk at you if you were not listening, of the dances with the girls' school nearby in the gymnasium and my first shyness at dancing and then my great enjoyment of it when I found I did not make such a fool of myself as I thought I would, of cool evenings on the wooded path along the river which swirled in countless eddies, all swept downstream by the irresistible current. I recalled memories of the Cape and its golden swamp grass with tips bent over by the salty breeze rendering a silvery gloss, as a hand brushes across a velvet cloth changing the reflecting angle of light, and the cranberry canning factory at the foot of the bay which was separated from the roaring ocean by sand fingers, and the winding asphalt roads lined by stately pines with their soft, refreshing scent, and the surf on the other side which pounded the sands with the relentless hammering of a judge's gavel demanding order of an angry crowd.

Such pleasant and dreamy and sweet-smelling memories faded as I fell into a restless doze in which I was half conscious of continually changing my position on the stones and brushing aside the land crabs which crawled out of the rocks and over my face. I dimly heard the occasional crack of a grenade being thrown, then the explosion, and the shrapnel humming through the air — a few Japs sneaking around in front of our lines — that's the way to keep 'em off, use grenades — good — the men knew their stuff — don't fire your rifles and machine guns until you can hear the Japs distinctly and know that they are attacking — don't let 'em know where our guns are located — wait until they hang up on our barbed wire — goddam these crabs. I thought I felt a slight breeze relieving the closeness of the night It was a shame about Woody — I wonder if he knew he'd get it — no, I was just reading into him — it was strange that he should have instructed Stramel back in the states when he was a corporal and Stramel only a private then — the two were certainly glad to see each other — and now well, I hope Stramel's OK. And I had heard a rumor along the line that Schmittou had been stuck with a bayonet — couldn't believe it — not Schmittou who was pretty good with his Tommy gun. Another explosion and whine — hope that one got a couple of 'em — I had seen Bennett very solemnly sitting in a shell hole looking at a picture while bullets were clipping the brush around him.

"What are you doin'?" I asked him.

"Lookin' at my wife's picture wonderin' if I'll ever see her again."

I was chuckling over that one — shocked by Koval's death — been over here twenty-eight months and slated to go home after this — he had been wounded in the arm and while going back to the rear got a bullet through his stomach — somebody saw him staggering on, holding in his guts with his hand, and McNeel and Winsor and Graham and Luciak and Stacheki; and so many others also were to go home after this one — and I was supposed to go home. Could I still find my way around New York? — almost unbelievable to see Fifth Avenue again, to buy a newspaper at Whalen's, ride the Eighth Avenue subway and the Staten Island Ferry when the sky is ocher and overcast and see the harbor with its green swirling tides and yellow foam and the towering gray skyline beginning at the Battery and spiring as far as the eye can see and smell the coal and oil smoke and feel the stampeding, pulsating, bawling, uproarious spirit of the city — then I must have slept.

The crack of a rifle made me rise up, fully awake. There was long silence. I listened very intently but heard no sound. I screwed my helmet around on my head and lay back once more on the bed of stones. I looked at my watch; the luminous dial showed eleven thirty-five. I noticed that here and there the clouds had broken and stars were blinking through the openings.

LaCoy was calling Sellers softly over the radio, hoping that it would work in a possible change of atmosphere. But all that the batteries could pick up was martial music. It was the second time the Japanese had jammed the air, the first having occurred the morning when Sellers was trying to call the second platoon. A woman had broken in, jabbering incessantly, drowning out his call. He bellowed through the mouthpiece.

"F— you, you bitch! Git off the air!"

The woman continued to jabber.

LaCoy remarked to me several weeks after we left Peleliu that during battle when he found himself stationary for any length of time he frequently felt a warning from nowhere to move. He always obeyed that feeling. In one instance he was sitting behind a rock on the Point and suddenly felt this urge. No sooner had he jumped to another spot when a bullet snapped into the rock exactly where his back had been resting. I have experienced the same thing several times. I was on the Point in a hole among the rocks, and for no reason at all other than a quick hunch I moved thirty yards away to another one. Immediately a mortar shell burst about five feet from where I had left. The shrapnel flew alarmingly near to my new position but did not touch me.

Premonition of danger is a definite thing. When all your senses are alert you can feel its approach. On patrol through jungle trails where you are liable to meet Japs head-on, where they wait in ambush, where they bivouac, you can feel when they are near. A sharp, prickling sensation runs up your back, you slow down your patrol and approach with infinite caution and silence. It is similar to that feeling when you are sure that someone is looking at you but you cannot see him. Something happened to Hahn on the Point which is like it He came up to two friends who were resting by a Jap pillbox. He sat down to talk with them when he suddenly felt himself alerted by this premonitive feeling. He stood up quietly and approached the exit of the pillbox. Inside he saw five Japs dressing wounds on their legs. He sprayed them with his Tommy gun.

Hand grenades were bursting in rapid succession. The explosions were muffled in the woods where there were gullies and small miscellaneous ridges. Then much louder bursts — approaching our lines — closer — and I heard the cry "Corpsman!" Jap mortars, big stuff, were pounding in the middle of us. Shrapnel was clinking across the rocks. We could only hold and take it, and there was nothing to fire at but the impenetrable black of the woods. The Japs were probably trying to soften us up for an attack. If we could live through the barrage we would be waiting for them. Wham, Wham, Wham, awful thumping along our lines.

"I'll be damned!" Jarvi was muttering, "that one got me in the thigh." He put on a bandage.

"Cut me in the arm too," Sovik was swearing, "it's hot as hell."

The fury increased. Flares swished up horn the rear. Sellers was shooting blind — I followed the cometlike streaks through the sky, and as they passed over my head I prayed they wouldn't break over our own positions and light us up like a Christmas tree. But they burst into flaming sparks well in front of us, flooding the woods with orange light — good work, Bull! — he had hit the range on the button.

"There they are. I see 'em, I see 'em!"

"We'll plug the bastards, don't look at 'em!"

A machine gun fired a burst, another one — it opened up with a vibrating roar, BAR's and rifles and grenades chattered in a wild medley.

Then it was dark. White muzzle flashes spit into the black. The noise increased as the Japs answered and their bullets spattered on the rocks and ricocheted in every direction and their mortar shells thundered into the coral raising a stink of gunpowder. Sellers was shooting more flares. They would keep the Japs down. The roar of the fight gathered new strength. Our tracers cut flaming trails through the woods, and then suddenly the Jap mortar sheik stopped falling; were they closing in for the assault? And as quickly our fire ceased on the left, on the right; in the center it continued for a moment There was utter silence. The smell of powder smoke hung over the rocks.

The woods were grim and ominous, and sometimes we could hear faint scuffling in the rocks and the underbrush. Flares revealed nothing. We fired short bursts and threw grenades at the sounds. Except for that and the pleading, sometimes angry cry, "Corpsman!" the night remained quiet

At the first sign of daylight the Japanese suddenly renewed their activities with such intensity that an assault seemed almost certain, and we soon understood the sounds that we had heard during the night. Snipers swarmed in the trees and bushes all around us, and from a long dip in the ground about thirty yards in front of us came barrage after barrage of grenades and mortars. We could see the Japs bob up quickly, catch the fling of their arms as they hurled. Below in the rocks we presented excellent targets for the Japs in the treetops. Almost before I knew it we were engaged in a blistering fire fighting with our backs to the ocean.

Thank God for the baseball we had played once! The throw to first base from the hot corner; the peg home from center field; our grenades were smashing into the gulley — long, high heaves in quick succession with every ounce of a man's strength behind them. Our machine guns raked across the draw riddling any Jap that stuck up his head. I saw a hand rise to throw a grenade. Our bullets reduced it to a bloody stump. But their mortars were firing faster. I heard the snap as they were discharged — wondered where they would strike — explosions along the lines —

the Japs had the range. A larger gun opened up, and the shells spread pink smoke as well as shrapnel. We were spraying the trees. The fight became a vicious melee of countless explosions, whining bullets, shrapnel whirring overhead or clinking off the rocks, hoarse shouts, shrill-screaming Japanese. Faces were gray with coral dirt and the smeared remains of the camouflage paint. Hibbard ran by to pick up a BAR from a man who had slumped over with a bullet in his chest I caught a glimpse of his face — chalked with dust, blue eyes almost turned black, dark circles under them, creases around his mouth, Knight was smiling — dark, roughly chiseled, Indian face — Hunter standing over Kuld's body just for a moment, strangely meditative, I remember — Kuld, big and red-headed and freckled, as calm in death as he had been in life with blood at the corners of his mouth — Beazley, his side ripped open by a grenade — our trousers torn by the sharp coral — water supply low, our lips and tongues parched.

"Hello, five, this is control. Hello, five, this is control. Do you hear me, over?" LaCoy was trying to get Sellers. If he did I would holler for reinforcements — they could bring them up by tractor. We needed them — badly — no answer the air was as dead as a morgue. Then Haggerty was volunteering; his red hair had turned sandy with dust — eyes like black needle-heads.

"Yes, Hag," I shouted, "go ahead. Get through. Bring some more people up here — anybody, I don't give a damn. Hurry and take care of yourself!"

"I'll bring 'em up!" he yelled, and climbed down the rocks to the beach.

Casualties were mounting fast They ran past me down to the shelter of the beach shelf, holding bloody arms, with red dripping down their legs, cursing their luck and the

Japs. Some were carried down on sagging stretchers. I smelled the powder vapor, acrid, choking, could see it swirling white — sweat in my eyes, stinging — jacket was wet on my back — rock chips spattering at my feet Jap stuff kept coming Jesus! why didn't they assault? — then we could knock them down like tenpins. They were dodging in and around the rocks in front of us — closer now — wiry little bastards — bandy-legged. I saw Hunter standing up throwing a grenade. As his arm swung forward he ducked and bullets crackled on the rocks over him. He stood up with his rifle at his shoulder and fared three shots. Suddenly he whirled around, his rifle flew up, and his helmet was rolling on the rocks. I saw blood streaming down his face.

"Hell of a lot of 'em out there," he was saying. "I got that mortar with my last grenade, but I missed the bastard that hit me. Just a graze on the head; I was lucky." He ran down below the cliff. I saw Willis and Lees next to me, crouching behind a rock.

"The line's getting awful thin," Willis observed, "looks like we'll have to draw in and tighten up."

"But that'll mean pulling back about twenty yards, and the Japs will move in on us covered by these boulders. We would be worse off then than we are now."

"Yeah, once they get in among these rocks here we're through." A Jap grenade struck a boulder, rolled and clinked down to within three yards of us.

"Another dud," Lees remarked casually, "we've been getting a lot of 'em."

Roderick, white as a ghost, jumped behind the rock with a shrapnel hole in his back which pumped up blood in spurts. "Take it easy," Lees told him, "turn around and I'll fix you up." He placed a bandage on the wound tying it firmly across the shoulders. The blood seeped through the bandage. Willis was shouting: "We must get these wounded boys out of here! Where in hell is the tractor?"

More and heavier stuff throwing pink vapor — the din was increasing — I was wondering if we'd get out of this alive — we were surrounded — we must hold the Point — even if we —

I looked down the beach. There were no troops coming our way, no tractor. Mortar shells were crashing on the sand and the reef just below the cliff spreading shrapnel dangerously near to the wounded men who were lying there.

"Get in closer to the rocks!" I bellowed.

Over on the right McComas was gazing intently at a rocky rise about a hundred yards in front of him. His eyes were coal Hack and his muscular body was alertly straining forward. I remembered his immobility, strangely noticeable in the turmoil of the fight. A grenade was fixed on his rifle which rested lightly in his hands. With a catlike movement he suddenly disappeared from my view behind the boulders.

I heard Webber's voice, calm — Boston accent — saw his face, hawk-nosed and gray-eyed and smiling through dirt smears.

"McComas just knocked out the big mortar that's been hittin' us so hard. I think we've nearly cleaned 'em out on the right; there's a slew of dead Japs out there on the rocks."

I saw Devlin on the left standing upright on the line throwing grenade after grenade. His jacket was unbuttoned and flying out with his motions.

"There he goes!" he yelled, pointing with a long arm toward the woods. Hoffman, his face smudged with dirt and powder grime, stood up beside him, and his BAR was vibrating and spitting flashes. Then other men stood up on the rocks. Then more, in the center, on the right, firing faster, hurling barrages of grenades that hammered a resounding note of finality. I saw the backs of running Japanese.

I turned around and there was Haggerty coming toward me with his rolling gait and his baseball cap low over his eyes. He pushed the visor back. An unlighted cigarette was hanging from the left corner of his mouth, "I've got some men, extras from other outfits I found on the beach, and we laid a phone wire along the reef from Battalion."

"Good work, Red. Get 'em on the line. The Japs are falling back!"

Fifteen men were piling out of the Alligator onto the coral edge, and our wounded were taking their places. Stacked on the beach were cans of water and more grenades and bandages and sulpha drugs and morphine and stretchers. I picked up the phone and rang Battalion, but heard no rasping sound. The wire had snapped already.

Now, just after the Japs had pulled back, the line was quiet except for the occasional crack of a rifle. Powder smoke clung low on the rocks and curled in and out among the niches. The men were watchful, haggard; some had stubble under their chins, many had shed their jackets and were trying to cool themselves. The dirt mixed with sweat had ground into the skin, and several had scorching red rashes under their arms. Dark circles were prominent under their eyes which were bloodshot. They were talking in low, calm tones. I heard no bravado, no complaining, no hysterics, no irritable arguments. Every face seemed older than it should have been, more hard-bitten.

Rowe was sitting on top of a rock with his knees crossed. He wore his helmet cocked on the right side of his head as though it were a Stetson. He fingered his thin mustache musingly as he watched the woods and the rocks in front of him where dead Japs lay in brown heaps.

"Hello, Rowe," I accosted him, "how have you been doing?"

"Pretty well, Captain, pretty well," his voice was razor-edged, "except that I'm wonderin' how O'Brien is — whether he kicked off or not. A-a-a-ah," he spat, "when you see your buddy stiff on the deck with foam droolin' out of his mouth, his eyes poppin' out and his hands clutchin' at the air you feel like you could kill every livin' son of a bitch of a Jap from here to Tokyo. I got a few of those bastards out there but that's not enough. I wouldn't stake a hundred of 'em against Obie. Yeah, Captain, and it all starts you wondering — whether — well, that's war I guess."

Through every mind ran the same thoughts; we had lost too many good men; how long could it keep up? The Jap had laid off for a while, but he would hit us again; we were still out on a limb; would we get relief so we could sleep? would we die? — so what — and we were bitter mad at the Japs. We hated them, and we would kill them and keep killing them or we would be killed. If it hadn't been for him we would never have been on this goddam island in the middle of no place with all these rocks, the blasted heat and no water or chow.

CHAPTER SEVEN

TEN hours later when white naval flares burst in front of our lines the silhouettes of gnarled tree trunks reminded me of a picture of Stonehenge in the moonlight. There was the same chilly light, the same sentinel shapes. Haggerty said that it looked like a petrified forest. There was a dim mist which swirled around these forms rendering an almost supernatural effect. In the light I could see its movement, curling wisps of nearly transparent tails.

"Would you like a stretcher to sleep on, that is if you're not superstitious?" Giddons asked me. "I know a man who fell asleep on a stretcher and died on it without ever waking up."

"That's a cheerful thought," I said.

"I wouldn't sleep on a stretcher if I was paid to, unless it's by necessity," remarked Haggerty.

"I think I'll take a chance on it," I said. "It'll be better than the stones." I placed the stretcher on the most level spot I could find under a tree and lay down on it on my back, I saw the trunk of the tree rising up about thirty feet where it became a shapeless web of shattered branches.

"You know, Skipper," said Haggerty, "when I went back this morning to get help those people back there looked at me as though they had seen a ghost. They had just about crossed us off the list."

"We had a close call all right, but it'll be different tonight; we're well prepared for 'em."

It would be our turn to throw heavy stuff: mortars and artillery. We had seven machine guns on the line and thirty more men. Radios were working, and there were two telephone lines to Battalion. For the first time since we landed I felt secure. Let the Japs come —

Five hours ago — the remaining ten men of my second platoon had joined me. Young Wiginton's round face was wreathed in a smile. He was the first to step out of the tractor.

"Gawsh! Captain," he said, "we're sure glad to see you. We was worried about you all up here and heard that you had been killed."

"We were worried about you too, Wiggle, you must have had a rough time."

"Yes sir, we got shot up pretty bad."

Tractors were rolling up to us all day along the reef. They brought my mortar section from up the beach, big men, with the tubes and base plates over their shoulders and clover leaf after clover leaf of shells, who set up their guns among the rocks and organized a chain gang to lug the ammunition from the water's edge. They brought up Lieutenant Klopf with his artillery observation team and a radio to communicate to his gun batteries which were located several thousand yards to the rear. He pulled a map from his dispatch case, and we figured out the correct concentrations to cover the area in front of our lines up to six hundred yards.

"We'll put as much explosive in there as you ask for," he said.

"You're liable to have a busy night," I told him. "The Japs want this Point."

"Just say the word and I'll—"

The chattering of machine-gun fire on our right interrupted our conversation. I called Sellers: "What's going on on the right?"

"That's B Company tryin' to push into the gap. They're havin' a hell of a time. The Japs are still as thick as flies in there." That was the third company that had tried to fill up that hole and make contact with me. I heard the booming of tanks —

"I'd hate to be isolated up here for another night, Klopf."

Then I saw First Sergeant Schmittou stalking up the beach, gaunt and glowering. I waved to him, and in return he swung a long arm over his head. Drops of perspiration had caught in the stubble of his day and a half's growth, and his eyes gleamed jet black.

"Glad to see you, Schmittou, I heard you had been stuck with a bayonet."

"Stuck with a bayonet!" he shouted. "It'd take more'n a goddam bayonet to get me. But them mortars nearly did it. Them bastards had me straddled to ten yards."

"Any of you hurt?"

"Wai, jest Mr. Stramel and I got outa there. The others'd been picked off before by snipers. I was layin' there jest where you left me, behind the bush. Mr. Stramel was back in the hole. Then this mortar drops twenty yards to my left, then twenty yards to my right, and I says to myself; Schmittou, the next 'un's got your number on it, and that son of a bitch lands ten yards in front of me. Before I knew it I'm jest about buried by sand and I looks back to see if Mr. Stramels OK and his face is stickin' outa the sand just as gray as I've seen, but he wasn't touched."

"How have the others made out back there?" I asked.

"Little 'Smitty' is dead, and Haber got it in the legs. The cooks were all Wounded when their tractor was hit by a forty millimeter, and Sutkaitus was run over by his tractor and had his legs crushed."

"Did he die?"

Yeah, he died. I seen a bunch a our guys lyin' on the beach. Seemed that most of 'em were from K Company."

The men in the tractors brought cheerful word. Swiftly it passed along the line spreading encouragement. "They say the airfield's been taken."

Sniper fire bothered us all day. Japs were sneaking around our lines and occasionally I heard the burst of a grenade. McComas, deciding to catch some sleep, told his men to keep a careful watch, lay down and closed his eyes. When he woke up an hour later he found a man who had fallen into a doze. He kicked him in the foot

"Goddammit!" he bellowed, "you cork off like that and some Jap will sneak up on ye. How d'ya know there aren't any Japs around here?" He swept his arm in a broad gesture. By chance it stopped when it pointed at a clump of bushes twenty yards out. Looking down his arm, he continued: "I'll run you up fer —" He stopped, staring at the bushes. "Well Jesus," he said, speaking slowly with a tone of amazement, "there are some Japs in those bushes." He crouched forward searching the spot intently with sharp eyes, and without saying another word slipped off into the woods. Three cracks of a rifle and a grenade burst followed very shortly. McComas returned with two more Japs to his credit.

Sporadically mortar shells dropped into us. When they pounded along the line they never failed to clip someone. Rarely was the rocky ledge down at the water clear of wounded men with blood-soaked bandages awaiting the next tractor. I remembered Humplik, pale as a sheet, splattered across the chest and arms by shrapnel, murmuring as if in a dream: "G'ese it's hot, g'ese it's hot, fan me, Mac, fan me, fan me, it's hot as hell." Schmittou fanned him across the face with a folded map.

"Fan me more, Mac, fan me more, I'm on fire. Fan me harder."

I had seen so many of my men killed or wounded that I was left benumbed. Seeing them fall right and left had become a regular part of a day's work. Death was as common as head colds, and the wounded were simply ineffectives who must be replaced and carried off the field at once. My own actions had become those of a machine, as though my muscles and mind had been trained and co-ordinated since my birth to perform mechanically the activities of fighting, at the mere fall of a switch. I had long since forgotten about fatigue, the soreness of my eyes, the sun blisters on my lips, the heat, the blinding glare of the rocks, and the fantastic nearness of death which I accepted as I would the danger of crossing a city street.

Down by that ledge I kept my radio. Lockhead, the operator, a young, smooth-faced kid with freckles, moved twenty yards down the beach with it seeking clearer reception, when the heaviest mortar barrage since early morning thundered about us; and Lockhead was caught out there on the sand. Lyons was yelling at him:

"Run back here, chicken, come on back!" The impact of the explosions shook the cliff, and loose coral tumbled down to the water's edge.

I was on the phone talking to the colonel. Trouble shooters had fixed the break in the line.

"Heavy mortars falling — coming from about three hundred yards to our front."

"OK, George, I'm calling for planes now."

Lyons was shouting again:

"Get the hell back here, Lockhead!"

Behind me was the pillbox which Willis and Anderson had knocked out. The Japs inside were fried black, and the whites of their eyes shone in the dark like phosphorus. The forty-millimeter gun was twisted and yanked cockeyed from its mount. The flame had scorched its blued surface to a dull gray. Lockhead had not heard Lyons and had remained there huddled behind a round stone. I saw his mouth moving as he pressed it against the mouthpiece of the radio. The mortars were still falling —

I heard the deep hum of engines approaching nearer, increasing to a roar. Gray planes with stars on their wings zoomed low over our heads, skimming the treetops, I heard the crackling of their guns spitting bullets which snapped above us and strafed the ground three hundred yards in front of our lines. The earth trembled with the impact of bombs —

Then the mortars ceased; Lockhead was miraculously unhurt, but once again I heard the cry, "Corpsman!" echoing among the rocks.

It was in the early afternoon that I sent out Daily and Hahn with their squads to patrol in front of our lines and attempt to discover the Jap strength and activities. They had moved only a hundred yards when the Japs, swarming out of the caves among the ridges, opened up with grenades and rifles.

Standing on the line anxiously watching the fight which ensued I felt ridiculously helpless. To commit more troops would weaken my flank on the right, exposing us to an attack from that direction, and I did not want to engage all my men in a pitched battle out there where the Japs had the advantage. We could not fire from the line for fear of hitting our own men.

"Cover those men," I shouted to the machine-gun crews, "but do not fire!" That was all I could do. It was not much.

Again I heard the rattling of rifle fire and the popping of grenades. Japs were bobbing in and out of the rocks — I could see their flat, brown helmets. At times it was hard to distinguish them from my men, so quick were the movements. Daily was running back, dodging from tree to tree, his leg soaked with blood and his trousers ripped. He was bringing his squad back man by man. So was Hahn on the right, with his arm dripping red.

Daily's dark, heavy-browed face was chalk-white when he spoke to me. He knelt down supporting himself with his arms pushed stiffly into the ground. He talked in gasps.

"There's a mess of 'em in the caves — take a hell of a lot of men to rout 'em out. Cushman's dead out there — got it in the head — had to leave him — got the others back all right."

"Good job!" I said, and told him to get in the Alligator which, fortunately, was just pulling up on the beach.

And Hahn brought his men back with one other casualty outside of himself. A corpsman cut the sleeve off his jacket. His atabrine complexion tad paled, and his eyes had dark rims around them.

"The boys are bringin' Jack down the beach — he's all right, I think — grenades and bullets flyin' all over the place. Looks like the Japs are concentrating around them knolls and gullies." Hahn followed Daily into the tractor.

I rang the phone. "Hello, Colonel, still plenty of Japs up front of us seem to be gathering for something — maybe a night attack — I'm going to harass them with mortars and artillery."

"All right, all right — has B Company made contact with you?"

"Not yet."

"Hell, they should have been up there by now."

One hour after this conversation a patrol reported that friendly troops were closing in on us, and by nightfall my right was firmly spliced to B Company's left. After thirty hours we were no longer isolated.

Lying on my back on that stretcher and thinking about the day that had just passed, I became more aware than ever of how close we had come to complete annihilation. In the early morning we had been reduced to about eighteen men, surrounded on three sides, with our backs to the ocean. If the Japs, who outnumbered us twenty to one, had rushed us — I shuddered at the thought The Point would have been lost and the beach would have been at the mercy of the Jap guns. I was sure that some unknown power must have been on our side. And I was mighty proud of my men and their sheer guts and stamina.

I was wondering if Anita realized somehow where I was and what I was doing. I knew she was worried because she would not have received a letter from me for several weeks, and that always meant I was going into battle. Her fight against anxiety must be worse than mine against the Japs. It is frightening never to know — for sure — I thought of her, laughing and curling up her nose and shaking her long hair, her eyes aglow with a rich, contagious joy of living, her skin very white and a suggestion of freckles across the top of her cheeks — freckles — she disliked them — said the sun brought them out and her voice, musical, speaking the purest English — said "rahsberry" for "rasberry" — I liked to kid her about that — we were riding on the Long Island Railroad — the click and clack of the wheels on the track the murmuring of voices in the car — the smell of cigar smoke, of fresh newspapers the conductor opening the door to call out the next station — we were talking or sitting very quietly — peacefully — watching — thinking — always peacefully — and the houses and the tree-lined roads and the bridges and the street lights and the track crossings and the busses and the schools at recess and the automobiles which were going our way and seemed to be motionless and the beer joints and the switches and the stations with gold and yellow signs and the red-tiled roofs — all were sequestered and quiet and peaceful — then they drifted away from me into mist that grew thicker and thicker swirling and turning and sweeping these images with it in circles which became confused and senselessly intermingled —

I heard rustling at my head — crabs again, coming out of the rocks to annoy me — scratching at the stones and the thorny weeds — time went on, and I was unaware of it — I thought I heard the rustling — no — it was sharper that night — a creaking — louder —

That noise! it sliced into my thoughts and my half sleep. It had a meaning. Something had warned me — that creaking — more than that — a splintering —

Then I saw. I was paralyzed Not to move meant sure death, but I couldn't. Some appalling vise had gripped roe. That tree with the shapeless web of branches was falling! I strained and swung my left leg over my right and rolled with all my might off the stretcher onto the ground. At that very instant the tree crashed lengthwise along the stretcher exactly where I had been lying.

Breathless I lay there, astonished at the closeness of my escape. Had I realized what was happening one split second later I would have been mashed to pulp.

"What happened?" exclaimed Haggerty abruptly sitting upright

"This tree nearly killed me. Look at the stretcher. It's crushed and almost buried under the trunk."

"Someone must be doing a lot of prayin' for you, Skipper."

"Yes," I said musingly, "there's several prayin' for me. I'm beginning to think it must do some good."

"Do you think you'll ever sleep on a stretcher again?" put in Giddons with a short chuckle.

"No, I guess I won't, unless I absolutely have to."

"I hate to say I told you so," remarked Haggerty, grinning, "but those things are strictly taboo."

I could not help laughing as the affair assumed a comical aspect. I began scratching away stones to make a new bed when I was startled by a figure climbing over the rocks.

"Who's that?"

"Adams."

"Password?"

"Chevrolet"

"What do you want?"

"I want to speak to the captain."

I went over to him and saw that he was one of the replacements who came up in the morning. He was nervous about something.

"What's the matter, Adams?"

"Well, we've been hearin' voices just in front of our positions, and a kind of squirming and gagging as though someone was being stabbed. We think the Japs grabbed a guy who went out to see what the score was?"

"He went out to see what the score was," I repeated, surprised.

"Who was it?"

"I don't know, but that's what the fellas all say. And we could use a couple of more men around that BAR position. Ain't many of us there."

"OK, Adams, let's take a look."

We wound through the rocks about ten yards and entered the coral basin where the line jutted outward, following the course of the rocks. The coral glowed ghostly white and threw a gray tone on the faces and clothes of the men who crouched behind the boulders with their weapons resting on top. Their helmets cast black shadows over their eyes as though they were wearing masks.

"Goddam this rockpile," Adams muttered as he stumbled on the stones.

"Shut up there" — a loud whisper.

Toller was squatting behind his machine gun, peering over the barrel into the woods which rose against the sky in thick clumps like balls of black wool.

"Have you heard anything out there?" I asked him in a hushed voice.

"Not yet, but further along on the left the boys say they can. Think well get an attack?"

"I believe so. It's dark enough for one."

"We're ready for 'em; plenty of ammo and grenades."

Stretched on the coral were dead men who had stiffened in rigid positions. Dark liquid, which I knew was blood, lay in pools around them.

I picked my way through the stones along the line with Adams following me.

"Hear anything?" I whispered to a man I couldn't recognize in the shadows.

'Think I did — sort of excited jabbering."

"Ssssh —," Belizna, next to him, was whispering. There was a stirring to my left, and I saw an arm thrown forward, heard the snap of the grenade pin and then the explosion which reverberated in the woods. The noises were more distinct now whispered gibberish and low squeals of pain. The grenade must have hit some of them.

"They're there all right and pretty damn near," I heard someone murmur.

"Keep throwing grenades at 'em and don't open up with your guns till you can see 'em," I said softly and followed along the line to where Willis was sleeping very soundly.

"Wake up, Will," I shook him by the shoulder.

He sat up quickly, looking around.

"Yeah, yeah, what's the matter?"

"Japs milling around in front of our center position. Shift a couple of men over there to strengthen it."

"OK."

I heard Schmittou talking over the phone. "It's damn quiet up here. Feels like somethings gwanna happen."

I woke Stramel. "Better check your guns, Ray," and told Haggerty to call his gun position and have the crews stand by.

I sent a runner over to Klopf with the word to be ready to cut loose his artillery; and up behind a big rock I could see LaCoy, restless, and waiting to lay in with his mortars.

There was nothing to do now but wait for the attack, if it was to come. I thought of the tree that nearly crushed me, an ominous beginning of a night's work.

The battle broke with a tremendous, angry roar as though a fiendish blast had shattered the doors of hell and exposed to human ears the horrible turmoil which bawled and writhed within. At the one hoarse cry, "There they are! They're comin' in on us!" the entire line opened up simultaneously, bursting into an uncontrolled din that stirred the most furious, savage instincts of a man. I found myself bellowing until I thought my lungs would crack.

"Give 'em hell! Kill every one of the bastards!"

The Japs were answering with grenades and mortars and rifles. Again I heard the whirring of shrapnel and the whine of bullets, many of which were smacking into the rocks, ricocheting and burning crazy trails in the air. The Japs were assaulting us with stampeding fury, wave after wave, charging blindly into our lines and the hail of bullets and shrapnel which we poured into them. Above the uproar I heard their devilish screams, "Banzai, banzai!"

"Klopf!" I yelled, "cut loose! Fire until I tell you to stop!"

"LaCoy! LaCoy!"

"Yes!"

"Let 'em have it! Traverse the whole line and keep firing!"

"OK!"

I went to Haggerty. "Red, put as many rounds in there as you can pump out." He was on the phone in an instant, shouting his fire order.

Now we had the power. We were on the giving end of this stick — seventy-five millimeter artillery, sixty and eighty-one-millimeter mortars, firing at will.

The earth shook under this new weight.

Shells crashed into the rushing Japanese and against the trees, spreading deadly chunks of shrapnel. The violent concussions rocked my senses. Barrage after barrage drummed a ruthless rhythm to the steady roar of machine guns and BAR's and the sharp popping of grenades.

"Artillery falling short!" The cry made me shiver — Rounds were landing twenty-five yards in front of the line — too close — I saw the fiery blasts as they struck.

"Goddammit, Klopf! Lift the range two hundred yards!"

"Short rounds! We're raising it now!"

It was all right. Klopf was doing a fine job.

I ran over next to LaCoy and heard him shouting into his radio. "Range 150, right 50, fire for effect. How many rounds did I say? — Fire until I tell you to stop!"

A voice in front of me was challenging someone: "Who's there?"

"It's LaBerge, it's LaBerge,"

"Who's there, I say? I'll shoot"

"It's LaBerge, goddammit, don't you know me? I'm LaBerge!"

Bang! I heard the report.

LaBerge roared. "Are you satisfied now, you son of a bitch, you did shoot me?"

Dammit, I said to myself — confusion — some nervous kid probably one of today's replacements who doesn't know anybody here — shot LaBerge through the shoulder.

A cruiser was throwing out flares, but the smoke of our firing hung around us and obscured our vision. The noise of the battle thundered on with greater momentum. The stench of the powder stung my throat making it raw. I suddenly realized I was soaked with sweat that was itching my eyes. The palms of my hands were wet.

I heard ferocious cries on the left at the water's edge. By the white light of a flare I saw the silhouettes of two figures, dim and queerly distorted in the battle fog, struggling against each other on the crest of the cliff. Their arms were swinging wildly, their heads lowered and legs intertwined. The largest figure seemed to heave forward with his entire right side. The knees of the other tent back, he turned sideways and losing his balance tumbled off the cliff. Then it was dark —

Henn ran in front of me shouting: "They're comin' around the flank in the water. Bring that gun down to the beach!"

"LaCoy!" I yelled, "drop some rounds along the beach fifty yards in front of us."

Shadowy figures moved swiftly by me carrying a machine gun and disappeared down the cut to the beach.

The artillery and mortars were still firing into the woods; the artillery further out now, more distant and rumbling. I heard no wild Jap victory screaming, only howls of pain rising out of the smoky night like animal noises. The firing along the center and right of our line had-dwindled, but on the left, as it countered a new threat, it picked up with new strength.

The Japs were cut down as they attempted to attack in the water along the reef. They were driven into the niches which indented the rocky cliff. There they were protected from hand grenades and bullets, so we threw thermite grenades into the indentures. The Japs caught fire and screeching horribly, with the ammunition in their belts exploding like strings of fire crackers, ran into the water and rolled over and over attempting to extinguish the flames which clung to them relentlessly. But that did no good, and they burned in the water, crackling human bonfires that lit up the night. Their shrill screams resounded so piercingly that I realized that the noise of battle had suddenly ceased.

Susinka came running over to LaCoy. "There's a pocket of Japs in a gully about fifty yards in front of me." He pointed with his arm. "I can hear them talking in there. They've got a mortar that's been firing at us."

"I'll put out a few more rounds."

Again that hollow pop as the shell left the tube, the vicious snap of the impact on the ground and the resounding explosion; one following another in rapid succession. After the last burst we heard squeals and sobs of pain which lingered for a few moments and then died out. We listened for other Japanese sounds, a shout, a rustling, a jabbering, a scraping of feet on the rocks. We heard nothing.

Our line was quiet and once more seemed to be smoldering under the powder smoke. Again I heard the water lapping against the rocks at the foot of the cliff. The battle had ended almost as abruptly as it had started. In front of us the woods were dead.

Now, when the artillery had ceased firing and the mortar men were resting by their guns and the men on the line were watching for any other movement, a stillness fell over us, a stillness of waiting for the dawn.

It came very soon. Gray and stark, the daylight crept over the woods and rocks. Flat streaks of black clouds stretched across the sky like steel bands, and the ocean, reflecting the mood of the new day, was somber. The air, still mingled with the smell of gunpowder, dripped with murk.

On the beach some of the men with their jackets off were cupping the salt water in their hands and throwing it over their faces and chests. Others were fumbling with cans of meat and beans and eating the mushy contents with their hunting knives. The watches on the line were sitting on the rocks with their rifles across their knees looking into the woods at the devastation which lay there.

The movements of the men, as they opened "C" ration cans, washed themselves, or poured water from the water barrels into their canteen cups, were slow and almost benumbed. They walked and moved their arms in a dazed way, and their minds seemed barely able to control the motions of their limbs. They preserved the calm that they had shown the first morning; the same quiet and rocklike attitude toward suffering and death; the same sturdy, undemonstrative feeling of pride and satisfaction in themselves and their company; the same loyalty, that they had not let themselves or each other down; the same bitterness over the losses of their friends.

That night we had suffered less than before. The wounded were lying on the beach waiting for the tractor which I could see was making its way toward us. I counted the men I had left. Out of the original 235 who had landed there were only 78 who had not been either killed or wounded. The Japs had accounted for 157 of us, but they were thoroughly beaten, and out in the water, on the beach, in the woods and on the rocks we counted over five hundred of them — dead.

Along the shore Jap dead washed in with the tide and bled on the sand. Out further on the reef we could see them floating and bobbing aimlessly with the motion of the water, some of them caught on the obstacle stakes they had driven there.

In the countless gullies and basins in the coral Jap dead lay four deep, and on the level stretches they were scattered in one layer. They sprawled in ghastly attitudes with their faces frozen and lips curled in apish grins that showed their widely separated teeth and blackened gums. Their eyes were slimy with the green film of death through which I could see an expression of horror and incredibility. Many of them were huddled with their arms around each other as though they had futilely tried to protect themselves from our fire. They were horribly mutilated;

riddled by bullets and torn by shrapnel until their entrails popped out; legs and arms and heads and torsos littered the rocks and in some places were lodged grotesquely in the treetops. I noticed one Jap in particular with both legs and one arm shot off, blasted naked, and a pair of horn-rimmed spectacles still resting on his flat nose; and another one who was a major, sitting placidly on a rock in the attitude of Rodin's "Thinker." He must have been nettled by the tactical situation which had developed, and while he had been trying to think it out, a bullet had penetrated his skull.

A sickening, putrid stench was emanating from the ones we had killed yesterday. Their yellow skin was beginning to turn brown, and their fly-ridden corpses still free of maggots were already cracked and bloated like rotten melons. Along the trail which led directly to our lines was a forty-millimeter gun half falling out of a crate and surrounded by the mangled remains of bodies. Blood had dripped on the barrel which was shining dully in the dreary light filtering through the trees. Seeing this I could think of no more scathing and ironic symbol of their disastrous efforts to drive us from the Point.

I was opening a can of rations when Lyons appeared and told me I was wanted on the phone.

The colonel's voice crackled over the wire.

"I Company will take over your positions at eight o'clock and continue the advance. You will go into reserve and get a rest."

Reserve! — rest! — the words sounded too good to be true.

The wounded were being carried into the tractor which had just arrived. Among them was Duke who had wrestled with the Jap on the edge of the cliff and hurled him down on the jagged rocks below. His leg had been slashed by a samurai sword. He had been lying in his foxhole when he had suddenly felt this hacking on his leg. Then a bullet had pierced his arm. He had roared with pain and rage and had jumped up engaging the Jap in the fierce conflict which I had seen momentarily through the battle smoke. There was Fox who had been stabbed in the shoulder and clubbed on the head by a Jap who had sneaked behind him among the rocks. In the nick of time he had swung his rifle around and drilled through the chest the Jap whose arm had been raised for the finishing blow. He had lain in the water, bleeding, stunned, until at the crack of dawn Byrnes waded over the reef and pulled him back to safety.

And I heard about Belizna who had felt something solid and pointed smack him in the chest. He had thought he was shot, but he could feel no blood, no sharp pain. When dawn broke he saw a dud grenade lying at his feet in front of him.

I could see more tractors heading toward us and troops moving up the beach. Around me I was aware of increased activity. Another tractor was unloading pots of hot coffee, sandwiches, beans and fresh apples. The men were forming in a chow line taking the food in canteen cups and empty "K" ration boxes. I heard the first sergeant.

"Now goddammit! if you people can't stay in line and keep spread out ye won't git any chow!"

At the foot of the cliff I saw Willis and Panarese stretching out in the water. I chuckled — guess they did not mind the dead Japs. Lees brought roe a cup of coffee and some doughnuts and an apple. I smoked a cigarette, and it felt cool and relaxing.

The colonel and his staff arrived, and the doctor pressed a small bottle of brandy in my hand and a large can of alcohol to give to my men. Schmittou rationed it out at the end of the chow line. The brandy slipped down my throat hot and invigorating.

I Company moved in and man by man took over our positions. I began to feel a weariness that made me want to lie down and sleep and forget. The sun, burning through the sulphurous cloud bank, made me drowsy. My eyelids were heavy. I heard the word "Move out!" passed along I Company's line and saw a blurred image of them advancing through the Jap dead and disappearing over the ground rise two hundred yards away, toward 0-2. Many of my men had already found beds on the coral and had fallen asleep in the first postures they had happened to assume. Some were carrying our dead to the beach where they laid them down respectfully in a straight row. There were no sheets to cover them.

Vaguely I heard the colonel talking over the radio.

"We have moved out — my companies are now at —" The words drifted off — indistinguishable and fading — Stramel brought more sandwiches and coffee. He gave me a ham sandwich which tasted deliciously cool and fresh — from some LST he said.

I sat down and leaned back against a smooth boulder — surprisingly comfortable, I thought. I shut my eyes and listened sleepily to the sounds around me, feet scraping and scuffling on the loose coral, low voices that droned monotonously, the occasional distant boom of a naval gun, all mingling into gentle, lazy, lulling tones. Softly they stole away from me and hummed into murmuring echoes that were soon lost

EPILOGUE

A MONTH and a half later, back in our base camp, we who were alive and not wounded were slowly forgetting Peleliu. Our memories were wearing out talking and thinking about it. The precariousness, the suffering, the hardship and the gore of the battles we fought there were subsiding from our thoughts and feelings in favor of the pleasant reality of just being alive, and a little more; some good chow, a few bottles of beer, a game of basketball, baseball, the anticipation of going home or the chance to write home and say that we were safe and untouched, movies every night in an outdoor theater with coconut logs for benches, and time to sleep and rest and relax with the knowledge that there were no Jap in the vicinity. And for our lives we did thank God or fate or luck or whatever form the unknown might have assumed for different individuals.

For us time had swallowed up Peleliu. We seemed to have been there an incredibly long time ago; in fact it appeared inconceivable that we had ever been there at all. Sorrow and bitterness from losses of friends, so strong at first, was tempered by a practical philosophy that was inescapably in our minds. "Someone had to die. It was too bad that it was he."

Replacements for the dead and the wounded and the lucky ones who were due to go home were already living in our base camp when we arrived from Peleliu one day in a cold, slanting rain. Very soon these men would be incorporated in the activities and the spirit of my company, and almost before we realized it we would be a new unit constructed around a small nucleus of the old.

After a fortnight of rest there would be parades, inspections, and scuttlebutt would be as rampant as ever. Voluminous orders for training would come down from higher echelons; schedules would be drawn up; new equipment would be issued, and areas for maneuvers assigned to us and plotted on the maps. The pressure would be on, and once again we would learn and teach the business of fighting and build the company into a combat machine. Whether tougher or easier than Peleliu, the next campaign, another landing on another island, would mean that more of my men would he killed, maimed and wounded, and to minimize that fateful number, we would train harder than even the higher echelons would expect.

Then would come orders for D-Day and H-Hour, with maps of the objective and descriptions of the probable Japanese strength. And in the rain-soaked gullies, on the slippery ridges and rocky beaches of the training areas, around the crude tables in the mess hall and in the dim-lit tents, the final plans would be made. By a certain hour of a certain day, we would be ready. Thus the wheel would turn and we of Company K, a mere speck on the giant rim, would have no other choice than to put on our gear and again wind down through the coconut grove to the bay where the ships would be waiting.

A NOTE TO THE READER

WE HOPED YOU LOVED THIS BOOK. IF YOU DID, PLEASE LEAVE A REVIEW ON AMAZON TO LET EVERYONE ELSE KNOW WHAT YOU THOUGHT.

WE WOULD ALSO LIKE TO THANK OUR SPONSORS **WWW.DIGITALHISTORYBOOKS.COM** WHO MADE THE PUBLICATION OF THIS BOOK POSSIBLE.

WWW.DIGITALHISTORYBOOKS.COM PROVIDES A WEEKLY NEWSLETTER OF THE BEST DEALS IN HISTORY AND HISTORICAL FICTION.

SIGN UP TO THEIR NEWLSETTER TO FIND OUT MORE ABOUT THEIR LATEST DEALS.

Made in the USA
Middletown, DE
05 February 2020